Computers:
New Opportunities for
PERSONALIZED
MINISTRY

Computers:

New Opportunities for

PERSONALIZED MINISTRY

Kenneth Bedell
Parker Rossman

Judson Press® Valley Forge

COMPUTERS: NEW OPPORTUNITIES FOR PERSONALIZED MINISTRY

Copyright © 1984
Judson Press, Valley Forge, PA 19482-0851

Library of Congress Cataloging in Publication Data
Bedell, Kenneth B.
  Computers: new opportunities for personalized
ministry.
  Includes bibliographical references.
  1. Church work—Data processing—Addresses, essays,
lectures.   2. Pastoral theology—Data processing—Ad-
dresses, essays, lectures.   I. Rossman, Parker.
II. Title.
BV4400.B37   1984   250'.28'54   84-7127
ISBN 0-8170-1039-4

The name JUDSON PRESS is registered as a trademark in the U.S. Patent Office.
Printed in the U.S.A. ⊕

Acknowledgments

Parker Rossman and Ken Bedell wish to express appreciation to the organizers of the first "National Conference on Telecommunications, Computers and the Local Church" where both were keynote speakers, conducted workshops, and met many of the people whose practical experience has provided illustrations for this book. Bedell also acknowledges information from participants in many workshops he has conducted, especially those sponsored by the Center for Parish Development at Lancaster Theological Seminary.

Rossman wishes to express appreciation to the faculty and administration—especially the theological department—of Central Philippines University for the invitation to give a series of six lectures which constitute several chapters of this book. Other sections have been used as lectures at Ohio University, at Jaffna College in Sri Lanka, at the Educational Testing Service in Princeton, and at the 1982 assembly of the World Future Society.

Bedell acknowledges the support and understanding of his district superintendent, Howell Wilkins, and the congregations of the Bethesda and Grove United Methodist Churches in Preston, Maryland.

We cannot mention all the people who read chapters and made suggestions, but we especially thank Dr. Ellis Larsen, Dr. John Deschner, Dr. Keith Watkins, Dr. Judy Hinds, The Reverend Robert Cramer, Dr. Randolph Crump Miller, Dr. Sarah Little, and The Reverend Burton Everist. We both owe deep appreciation to our wives and to our most helpful and understanding editor, Harold Twiss.

Table of Contents

Preface

We live in a world that is rapidly changing. Some changes result from a logical progression of events: people walked, then rode animals, invented cars to move from one place to another, flew aircraft through the air, and now rocket to the moon. Other changes result from or cause a reexamination of the very direction of history: nuclear war is not just the next development in warfare; it threatens to destroy human life on earth. Computers are the next step in information processing: from writing to printing to electronic information processing. Computers also raise questions about the nature of intelligence and what it means to be human.

Should a church begin using a computer now? Should it follow Pastor Hopeful who sees potential for new technology and is willing to take some risks? Or should it delay like Pastor Skeptic who has not yet bought an automobile because he is waiting for the invention to be perfected?

The authors of this book usually side with Pastor Hopeful. But the purpose of this book is to encourage thoughtful discussion and more careful preparation for church use of computers.

Computers and related electronic technology are now available to churches and schools at such low cost that many are now buying computers without adequate advance study and preparation. This book, therefore, as a sequel to Ken Bedell's *Using Personal Computers in the Church*, is addressed primarily to people who now have access to a computer or who may obtain one soon. We offer here a larger view and more comprehensive list of possible computer uses. No parish, church school, or agency is likely to use all of the possibilities described here, but this overview can serve as a checklist for parish leaders, after they study their own work and program, to see where a computer might help. We hope that this book will also stimulate the imagination toward new programs and possibilities that computers might enable churches to do.

In any case, this book can help satisfy the curiosity of church people who buy, rent, or borrow a computer, answering such questions as: How are other congregations using such technology? What is possible and financially feasible in a church setting? There is no science fiction in this book. It reports only what some parishes are actually doing as well as what computer uses are possible with existing technology.

Computers and related technology are changing so fast that published advice is quickly out of date. Doing complicated tasks with a computer may soon be as easy as driving a car. This book is not discussing "the motor under the hood," but how one might use the technology in church work.

The authors bring varied perspectives and experience to this task. Bedell, pastor of small rural churches, reports ways in which he and his congregations actually use a computer in parish and pastoral work. Rossman has served on the staff of urban and large churches. He is an interdisciplinary theologian who for several years directed a Continuing Education of the Ministry program that helped over two thousand pastors evaluate their work and make plans to improve it. He directed a series of study conferences on "Theology and Imagination" in the 1960s. His was one of the first church programs ever to make extensive use of computers and related electronic technology.

Both authors were keynote speakers at the first national conference on the use of computers in the local church, and both have lectured in workshops and at theological schools on church computer use. Some of the ideas and experiences reported here have come from participants in such events and from the Church Computer Users Network of which Bedell is president. Rossman is preparing a sequel book, "Fish Seeing Fire: How Computers May Change the Shape of Religious Research, Thought, and Institutions''(working title).

In an effort to make this the first religious book prepared entirely with computer technology, Rossman, first in the Philippines and then in Connecticut, and Bedell in Maryland typed drafts on computer word processors, exchanged drafts via computer disks, and secured a publisher who would review the manuscript so that corrections could be made at a computer terminal. Type was then set directly from computer diskettes supplied by the authors. The money saved by not having the book re-typed for printing was shared by the publisher and the authors. This

```
    Word Processor      Column = 1      Row = 47

    June 6, 1984

    Dear Parker,

    The drafts of two chapters I sent you cost me $2.34
    in postage. Yet I can send you a computer diskette
    that will hold over half the book for 54¢ postage.
    So from now on I will send you diskettes with drafts
    and letters on them. You can either read the mes-
    sages on your computer screen or print them out
    on your printer.

    Sincerely,

    Ken
```

Sample of Correspondence by Computer

kind of electronic publishing may in the future greatly reduce printing costs. A publisher might print only the number of copies for which orders exist, and each small reprinting could then be easily corrected and updated so that the book need never become outdated or go out of print as long as it is useful.

The authors prepared the text on Commodore 64 computers, which were available in the fall of 1983 for $199, using WordPro3 brand word-processing software. Rossman replaced his Commodore 1541 disk drive ($299) with a MSD disk drive ($400) and used a Prowriter printer ($600). The Prowriter dotmatrix printer was used to prepare the manuscript for the publisher because it produced a better-looking page than Bedell's Gemini-10 printer, which had been purchased for $309. During the writing of the book, Bedell used a modem ($100) to obtain information from distant data bases and to communicate with other computer users.

The work of revision, making corrections, and rearranging text was much quicker and easier than with an ordinary typewriter; and such work, which often is a chore, became easy and pleasant. It was also possible to work late at night or very early in the morning on the silent computer keyboard without disturbing family members or neighbors.

This book does not attempt to answer questions about which computer or what software should be purchased by a church. But the appendices discuss ways that a church might approach the procedure of obtaining a computer system. The authors believe that a person rather than a book will be a better resource for an individual congregation considering computer use. Unfortunately, such well-trained church consultants are hardly available as yet and probably will not be until many more parishes begin to demand their assistance.

Until denominations and ecumenical agencies provide good standards, guidelines, and professional advice on computer use, most congregations will probably continue what they are now doing. They will buy a small computer or experiment with computers that belong to lay members. This book is for use at such a time of experimentation, although the authors hope it will also help to motivate more careful planning in the use and purchase of computers.

"I don't think religious groups will pass up the opportunity to use computers aggressively to achieve their goals," said Dr. Ronald Lien of the Control Data Corporation at a church conference on computer use. "There is a precedent for being aggressive in using communications technology. Gutenberg's printing press was used to make Christ's teachings available to the common people . . . bringing about a reformation . . . and enlightenment of the masses." And Thomas Sheridan of the Massachusetts Institute of Technology, speaking to a World Council of Churches conference at his school in 1979, urged church people to let computers do what they do well and to "celebrate ways in which people are not computers," because people are more adaptable and creative. Beware, he said, of the mystification of computers, of attributing magical properties to them. "Hold the designers and programmers accountable, not the technology itself."

So we focus in this book on how parishes might use computers well in the service of God. We see this book as but the beginning of an ongoing conversation and invite additional information and suggestions from computer users everywhere and questions from church people who find present answers inadequate. Of course we cannot answer all of the questions. No one can as yet. But we hope this book will contribute to the process of gathering and sharing information, experimentation, and evaluation, all of which in time can help provide good answers, excellent advice, and guidelines for parish use of computers.

Definitions

Computer equipment, called *hardware*—the physical components of a computer system, made of metal, plastic, and glass: a viewing screen (monitor); a typewriter keyboard usually on the box that contains the computer itself; an offline storage system (a floppy disk drive, hard disk drive, or less satisfactory tape recorder); probably a printer; perhaps a modem or extra terminals connected to a central computer.

CPU or *Central Processing Unit*—the part of the equipment that processes information.

Software, sometimes called *programs*—the set of instructions, written in narrowly defined computer language, that controls the operation of the computer.

Information, sometimes called *data*—can be anything that is put into symbols, such as letters or numbers. All information used by a computer must be translated into electronic symbols. This is usually accomplished by typing the information on a keyboard.

Disk drive—a recording device that makes it possible to store information on disks when the equipment is turned off and when the information is more than the CPU can store at one time.

Floppy disks or *diskettes*—circular sheets of plastic, coated with a special material that makes it possible for them to record electronic symbols. These can be inserted into a disk drive so that information recorded on them can be used by the computer system. More expensive hard disk drives use specially coated metallic disks that store much more data than a floppy disk.

Terminal—the typewriterlike keyboard and TV-like screen on which information is transmitted into and out of the computer.

Modem—equipment that allows one computer to communicate with another computer over a telephone line.

Data base or *data bank*—a library of information stored on a large computer's memory, available through a telephone line connected to a terminal.

Information utility—a vendor or company that connects a user to commercial data bases for a fee.

Churches Enter
The Computer Age

The church is going to computerize," boldly announces Pastor Hopeful.

His good friend Pastor Skeptic wonders, "Is that a good idea? Can computers help the church be more faithful to its purpose? Or will the purchase of computers simply use money that could better be spent on mission, time that should be used for evangelism, and energy that might be used to build Christian community?"

"You've pointed to the whole idea," Pastor Hopeful replies. "The church is going to use computers for mission, evangelism, and building community. With computers the church can do a better job of fulfilling its purpose."

"I've got a lot of questions," says Pastor Skeptic. "What can a computer do in a church today that cannot be done without one?"

Church Use of Computers

The advantage of computers—information processors that manipulate data according to rules established by the software (sometimes called programs)—is that they work very fast. Some tasks that otherwise would take hours or days can be accomplished in a few seconds. A computer can also work with very large amounts of information at one time. Computers, therefore, offer a potential empowering of the church to be more effective in some areas of work by reducing the amount of time and energy required. This is true only when large amounts of information are being used or when there are benefits from rapid manipulation of information; otherwise some different tools—for example, paper and pencil—may serve better to accomplish tasks.

For example, a chronological list of baptisms, with new ones regularly added, could be stored on a computer disk. When needed, the list could be printed out on paper. But what advantage is this over a chronological list in a ledger? For this chore the church does not need to use a computer.

There may, however, be ways that a computer could help a church make better use of the list of baptisms. With proper software, a computer list can be called up from the disk for sorting in a variety of ways. If an alphabetical list of baptisms should be needed, then using the computer to alphabetize and print the list would save many hours of church office time. The computer could also prepare lists of baptized persons between the ages of forty and fifty or those people who have July birthdays, if such lists were needed. However, electronic technology is useful for such tasks only to the extent that the data in the computer is regularly updated and only for tasks for which very clear rules for the manipulation of information are defined. That is, a computer can prepare a list of all baptized people with birthdays in July only if the birth dates have been entered into the computer system.

To use another illustration, it is impossible for the computer to answer the question of who is in the greatest need of a pastoral visit today. Yet if rules for visitation are established, they can be encoded in software which can then be used to propose a list. Such criteria might be: people who have experienced a crisis in the last two months, those who have returned from the hospital within the last ten days, those who have not attended church for five consecutive weeks. In order to present a list of these people, the computer also would require, however, that information be fed into it about church attendance, personal crises, and hospital stays. The result is not a list of those in the parish with greatest need of a pastoral visit but simply a list of the people who fall into certain categories defined according to the information that has been entered into the computer.

In every church there will be two kinds of computer applications: first, using a computer to help with information processing that is already being done; and second, gathering new information or using information in new ways. While some computer scientists are trying to develop what is called artificial intelligence—computers that think like human beings—the applications described in this book assume the use of the intelligence of people.

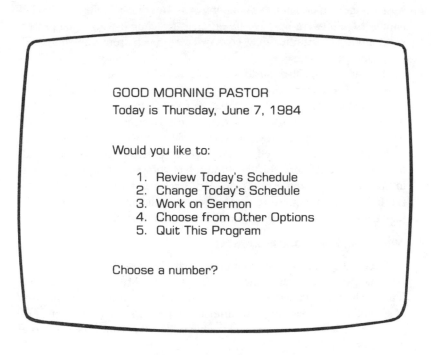

GOOD MORNING PASTOR
Today is Thursday, June 7, 1984

Would you like to:

1. Review Today's Schedule
2. Change Today's Schedule
3. Work on Sermon
4. Choose from Other Options
5. Quit This Program

Choose a number?

Sample Menu for Daily Calendar

Waste of Money?

Is a computer worth the expense? That issue can be resolved only by a study of how a particular congregation may make use of the equipment. The decision to purchase a computer now may be comparable to the situation of a pastor in the 1920s who wondered whether to buy a Model T Ford as a first car. Would we have advised him or her to wait for the Model A? Was a whole day spent transferring from bus to bus to make one hospital call that could have been made traveling a half hour with a car? Shall we ask church staff today to spend all day on a routine job that could be done in a half hour with a computer?

On the other hand, closets in many parish houses are full of hardly used technology: projectors, video cameras, tape recorders, and other equipment that a congregation may have purchased hastily. Good stewardship requires that waste be avoided and that church leaders beware of being hypnotized by the glamour of new technology. A church can waste money on computers in many ways. Too much equipment can be purchased. Software may not be efficient for church work. Equipment with similar capabilities may cost twice as much from one source as from another.

The church can also waste money if insufficient equipment is purchased or if service or help is not available when needed. Some business firms find that they must now replace computers that are only five years old. Others find themselves with long-term commitments to systems that were the best available when purchased but that waste money today.

Would the money be better used if given to help the poor? Or would the poor be better served if the church had computer equipment to use in making service and action more effective? Feeding the world's poor is ultimately a political issue, and we report in chapter 10 how computers may help the church become politically more effective on such issues.

When Computers Break Down

A second worry is about computer reliability. Do churches dare trust essential work to such vulnerable technology? Momentary electrical failure can result in serious information-processing errors and the loss of essential information. And almost anyone can tell of a recent experience in a store or bank when business was stalled because the computer was down.

The fact that cars break down, however, is not generally seen as a reason not to use them. Usually information will be saved in several different forms so that it can still be retrieved if the equipment fails. Extra copies of a computer disk can be made to serve as backups in case a disk gets damaged, just as one keeps a carbon copy of a manuscript. If a hard disk is used, then important information can also be saved on a floppy diskette, which can be stored in a safe place. Records that cannot be replaced should never be entrusted only to an electronic form but should also be printed out so that it would be possible to reconstruct them.

As we worked on this book, one of our disk drives developed a problem, and we learned that it could not be repaired in time for us to meet the publisher's deadline for completing the book. We were, therefore, faced with extra expense as we would have been had our car broken down on a journey. It is necessary to develop strategies that minimize dependence on a particular piece of equipment. A church might decide to buy an inexpensive typewriter-quality printer and also a faster dot-matrix printer so that the church work would not come to a standstill if one of the printers broke down. But the most important strategy is to make sure that both the equipment and the software are supported by competent service people who will make repairs quickly at reasonable cost.

Will Churches Use the Technology Well?

Computers can help churches cope with the information glut; yet computers can also add to that glut if proper precautions are not taken. Using computer and telecommunication technology, the church office could stuff the mailboxes of members or potential members with religious junk mail. Using a computer simply to generate more reports, printed pages, and mailings is not necessarily a good use of the technology. A computer's ability to generate reports can be used to confuse and overwhelm as well as to clarify. Paul Strassman has warned that in some organizations, for example, the wrong people are able to keep themselves in office by using computers to generate an unmanageable flood of redundant information.

There is also a danger that computers will be used only to control and manipulate people. Seymour Papert of M.I.T. shows how, especially in teaching, this tendency can become serious. Computers should be used creatively to help people learn to teach themselves and to control the technology themselves. In the church, care must be taken that each computer application is motivated by a desire to facilitate the legitimate work of the church rather than to manipulate people.

We know that people should not drive a car without proper instruction and that any technology which can harm people must be carefully used. And we must not forget—now that microelectronic computers are becoming cheap, plentiful, and more reliable—that their creative use will require imagination and great skill. It is necessary to beware of quacks and exploiters, also. The best defense against underused and misunderstood technology is to make sure that vision and training are given to the church people who will be using the technology.

Danger of Pursuing Popularity

American society has already decided to tolerate and encourage the use of computers to analyze opinion polls and other statistical information. Computer projections have become part of American life. Although one might argue the wisdom of having a computer-projected outcome of a presidential election announced before the polls open in

Hawaii, the direction of American society is set. We will see in the future more computerized opinion polls, more computerized analyses of information collected about individuals, and more computerized projections. The prestige of the pollster in a presidential campaign evidences the weight that opinion polls are given in the decisions made by politicians. Politicians have always asked: "By taking a certain stand will I increase or decrease my popularity?" But computer analyses of polling information claim to give politicians precise answers. A politician can choose to speak strongly about issues that are popular and ignore unpopular issues.

One might argue that politicians should reflect the attitudes and prejudices of their constituents but that the church is called to be faithful, not popular. Should a pastor in the future take into consideration a computer projection about the impact of prophetic actions on contributions to the church? Will the proclamation of the gospel be limited to what computerized polls indicate people want to accept or already believe? Will neighboring congregations compete for members the way that politicians compete for votes?

There is a danger that church computer programs will be used to answer a question that people in the church should never ask: What must we do to be popular? The church has been called to ask: What must we do to be faithful? And how can we respond in love to the needs of people?

Dangers to Privacy

Will confidential counseling information no longer be private if church records are computerized? We read horror stories about young people breaking into the computerized records of colleges, business firms, and government agencies. Military chaplains are warned that microcomputers are not suitable for processing classified information. Will the church computer also be vulnerable? Can any high-school student discover how much each person pledges to the church once financial records are computerized?

Most churches will be able to protect the privacy of members with computers as well as they do today without computers. But it will be necessary to take certain precautions. Churches may decide to buy their own computers to keep confidential information out of the data banks of other community institutions. Computerized financial records can be kept on a diskette—under lock and key—which can be as private as any other sort of record. Decisions may be made not to keep certain information stored on a hard disk, which offers a greater potential for unauthorized use. Software especially designed to control access to information may be used. Some software is designed to give information only to authorized persons and to warn when data is taken without authorization. And, in any case, most congregations are a long way from using the kind of interconnected computer networks that students have penetrated.

Discussion of the issues around the purchase of a computer may help church people become more aware of what to do about the computer-enabled invasion of their privacy which now occurs all the time. Concern for the privacy of church records needs to be considered in the context of a society in which a person's ability to get a job, credit, insurance, or education can be greatly reduced because of errors in information that is stored in a computer. The church needs to look closely at the ways information from the computer files of a hospital or from a police file about an antiwar protest can slip into the computer files of a bank or insurance company. A police officer warns that the use of computer technology by a service organization can blunt or sabotage its efforts unless care is given to developing a system that will really serve intended goals. As churches learn to take safeguards with their own computers, they will be better prepared to take initiative in insisting that privacy be protected in all computer use: local, state, national, or global.

Depersonalization and Dehumanization?

It would be a mistake for church people to minimize the possibilities for dehumanization and depersonalization that exist with the coming of information-age technology. Faculty members of the Department of Communications at Pennsylvania State University warn that our human ability to think straight and to talk clearly is deteriorating under the influence of electronic communications. Professor William Kuhns of the University of Ottawa points out that the image modern children have of the world is formed less and less by real experience; rather it is mediated more and more through computerized electronic technology. Real animals, for example, are replaced by the cute, computerized mechanical animals of Disneyland. Shall churches contribute to this trend?

Children do not get enough physical exercise if they ride everywhere in cars. So also their humanity, warmth in human relationships, sensitivity, and clarity of vision may be altered as experience is transformed and mediated to them by electronic technology. It is too early to know whether computers by their very nature do devalue human life as some critics have suggested. Rose Goldsen sees electronic technology causing desensitization and trivialization of emotional commitments. Fred Wilhelmsen and Jane Bret in *Telepolitics* worry that a new type of human being is being produced: a neurotic who demands instant satisfaction, who has less imagination, a terrible loneliness, less of a sense of history, and who is massively ignorant.

If society is going to become more passive because many people sit mindlessly before a computer monitor or videogame, then the church must find new ways of personalizing and humanizing. And it is clear that effort must be made to insure that church applications of computers affirm the value of human life. For example, although many of the first computer systems assigned a number to each person, number assignments are not necessary. The church computer should use people's names. The church needs to be vigilant to insure that computer reports do not encourage those in the church who would think of people as only statistics.

If churches take care, the computer can be limited to tasks that do not depersonalize any more than do the telephone, mimeograph, or car. One might argue that any of these technologies can depersonalize. Indeed, one pastor demonstrated that his ministry could be much more personal if he walked everywhere and talked to people in person instead of using the telephone.

With careful planning and sensitivity to the dangers of computer use, pastors can spend with persons the time saved by computer use. Meetings, too, can be much more personal and can be more sensitive to personal concerns when the computer assists in organizing agendas and routine details. Dehumanization and depersonalization are problems throughout modern society. So churches, whether they use computers or not, must be sensitive to and seek to deal with these issues.

Danger of Failing to See Dangers

"Twenty years from now," says Pastor Hopeful, "church leaders may well be amused by some of our worries about computers in the 1980s."

"However," Pastor Skeptic warns, "they may also be distressed that we did not take more precautions, that church people did not give more careful thought to preventive action in order to avoid some of the dangers and to solve some of the potential problems."

When church members first sit at a computer terminal, they may not realize that they are taking a first step into a new age, as did the astronauts in their first step on the moon. The TV audience held its breath when those first astronauts opened their spaceship door, because people had been warned of many things that could go wrong. Adequate precautions had been taken but only because of a willingness to admit that potential dangers call for great care. Jacques Ellul[1] and others have long worried that each new advance in technology—especially those that bring great hope—also involve potential dangers to humanity. As our society takes the leap into the information age, business, political, and even church leaders often seem content to improvise and deal with crises only as they arise. The foremost danger we face from computer technology, therefore, may be the result of inertia, our failure to anticipate problems and to develop long-range plans to deal with the stunning impact and changes that this electronic technology is likely to make upon the life, work, and thought of the church.

Again the analogy of the car may be helpful. We have been using automobiles for a half century; yet serious auto accidents each year hurt and kill more people than have major wars. Drivers sometimes get lost and then don't use cars as efficiently and carefully as possible. Our infatuation with cars resulted in the decay of public transportation within and between cities. Nor have we been sensitive to the dangers of cars increasing the carbon monoxide content of the air or the level of lead dust along the highways. The tragedy is not that cars were invented or became popular. The tragedy is that their limitations were not recognized earlier so that they could have been part of a rational transportation system that included public transportation in and between highly populated areas. Yet the drawbacks of the automobile have not prevented church people or churches from using cars. We hope that the use of computers in religion will take place with more intentionality.

Idol or Gift of God?

Some people worry that the church may become too dependent upon electronic technology and may even come to place idolatrous faith in it. But the church's faith must be in God, not in computers, and church people must pray for God's help in making good use of electronic technology.

Some people are already expecting too much of computers; they feel that information-age technology will somehow solve the world's and the church's problems. They read of computers that sometime may think better than human beings do, of predictions that computers will be implanted in human brains, and of other suggested interfaces between human beings and advanced computers. Some scholars worry that computers will lead people to think that human knowledge includes only that which can be quantified and handled by computers. Others, says Seymour Papert, fear that computers may lead to mechanical thinking to such an extent that people will begin to lose respect for their intuitions, values, and powers of judgment, that the computer will become the model of all good human thought.[2]

Some of these fears are understandable, and churches will make a great mistake if they allow the use and control of computers to remain entirely in the hands of secular and commercial forces. Those who can use computers may ultimately be able to control the way knowledge is organized and made available and the way education is conducted. It is therefore as essential for church people today to become heavily involved in computers as it has been for them to know how to read and write. If church people do not prepare themselves to enter the computer age faithfully and responsibly, then they may be surrendering to those who will abuse human beings and take freedom away.

The belief that computers may be used to make society more human and to help solve problems that may otherwise overwhelm and destroy humanity does not, however, assume they have special powers of salvation or that they have an ability to accomplish supernatural feats. Churches need to model a use of computers that does not assume that computers have special powers of salvation or the ability to accomplish supernatural feats.

Dennis Benson warns that computer use will have little constructive impact on the life of the church if it is not woven into the texture of the faith community's personal concern for each of its people. The youth of the church have enormous expertise in computer technology and can serve as resources for the clergyperson willing to ask for their help. Computer applications will be fresh and vital only if people take seriously God's gift of human interaction. In a strange way the computer age calls Christians to continue faithfully the traditional role of enabling the ministry of others. "It is ironic that a machine would call us to be more spiritual and sensitive to our people." Benson's approach to computer use requires that Christians "be more human in the presence of the computer than we have been in the past."

"It is our humanity and our spirituality which are really aroused by the challenge of this new medium. The advent of the computer shifts every part of our lives in such a way that all the other parts interface differently," requiring that new theological foundations be probed since "who we are and whose we are will determine the potential of the computer in our work."[3]

Dangers to Freedom and Human Rights

Professor Beverly Harrison of Union Theological Seminary, speaking at a church consultation on information-age technology, presented evidence that the use of computers continues and worsens the oppression of women, minorities, and the poor and that this will continue unless church people become sensitive to the danger and actively involve themselves to prevent such abuse. On the other hand, church computers and related information networks are already demonstrating the capacity for countering the domination of information by callous or insensitive commercial interests who, according to speakers at the 1980 Pacific Communications Conference in Hawaii, want to reserve computer communication facilities for themselves exclusively and do not intend to make access universally available. This restriction would mean the decline of democracy and the formation of a new, permanent underclass. Harrison said: "The problem of gaining access to public information grows worse daily, and the new technologies give ruling elites further means to assure passivity through ignorance, misinformation, and prejudice."[4] Most computer programs, she said, are developed for business, only secondarily for education. The heart of computer technology at present is in the military sector.

Professor Mary Alice White of Columbia University spoke of her concern that American society is being divided into those who are and those who are not computer people, with a new elite emerging in a way that restricts information and education for all. She said, "I would urge you [church people] to resist the notion that common ordinary people like you and me cannot understand the new [computer] technology. I resist the phrase 'user friendly.' . . . It's a real put down to people."[5] She urged resistance to the use of the phrase "lay people" when using it defers to engineers or refers to people unable to understand or participate in important aspects of the information age.

To surrender initiative because one feels he or she cannot learn surrenders power, perhaps even to demonic forces. Computers may indeed pose dangers to those who do not prepare to use them in human service. This is no time for Christians to drive into the future while looking in the rearview mirror.

Footnotes

¹ Jacques Ellul, *The Technological Society* (New York: Knopf, 1964).

² Seymour Papert, *Mindstorms: Children, Computers, and Powerful Ideas* (New York: Basic Books, 1980).

³ Dennis Benson, "FAKE CAT: Computer as Medium and Message," *Military Chaplains Review* (Spring 1983), pp. 65, 66.

⁴ "Education in the Information Age: The Role of the Churches," *Report of a Consultation* (New York: National Council of Churches, 1983), p. 10.

⁵ *Ibid.*, p. 11.

For More Information

See Gary Abrecht, "Defining Technological Change in Juvenile Courts," *Sociology of Work and Occupations* (August 1979); *Communications and the Future* (World Future Society); UNESCO, *Impact of Science on Society*, no. 2, 1983; James Botkin, "Innovative Learning, Micro-Electronics and Intuition," *Prospects*, vol. 12, no. 1; Kenneth Bedell, "Word Breaking," *Media and Values* (Summer 1983); Kenneth Bedell, "Introduction to Computers for Ministry," *Military Chaplains Review* (Spring 1983).

Checklist

A congregation's computer purchase and use should be founded on:

—a review of present and projected programs.

—a clarification of goals to be accomplished within specific church programs and areas of work.

—a study of how these programs can better be implemented, step-by-step, in order to determine where and how a computer could help.

—a review of privacy and justice issues and other concerns expressed by the congregation.

—a job analysis by professional staff and volunteers to determine where a computer might save time or help them do their work better.

—a quest for some new vision—that is, programs that have not been possible but which might be undertaken with a computer.

Computers for Study and Communication

Communicating the gospel, studying the Bible, and obtaining other resources for study can be facilitated for pastor and laypeople with computer use. New excellence can be possible in study and sermon preparation. Many church people think of using the computer only for office work, and many pastors have been slow to see how all their work as communicators, which is at the heart of ministry, can be improved and made more excitingly effective when a computer modem connects the church study with distant libraries and data banks. We will discuss the church office and some administrative uses of computers in the next chapters. But first, how does a computer affect pastors' studies?

Word Processing

First of all, using a computer as a word processor can facilitate the production of all the written material prepared in ministers' studies. Increased productivity and more free time for work that is otherwise neglected can result when the word processor replaces the typewriter. Someday soon a special electronic study desk will be available for pastors. It will serve as an electronic research and administrative staff. At this study desk a pastor will be able to refer to notes, search through large libraries of references, and prepare written documents. Already some pastors are discovering what a delightful help the computer can be with studying, at least in preparing sermons and papers.

Have you tried creative writing on a word processor? The words are first typed onto the computer keyboard, much as one types on a typewriter, but one sees what is typed on a TV-type screen rather than on paper. The computer stores the symbols in its memory and can be commanded to make changes in the material before anything is printed on paper. One can change the order of words and letters, delete or duplicate them, search through the document and make systematic insertions and deletions, and prepare the copy for printing. One can write and edit with much less effort than with a typewriter.

It is easy to correct typing, spelling, or grammatical errors on the screen by giving a command to insert, delete, or replace letters. It is possible to purchase word processing software that will instruct the computer to compare each word of your text to a list of words in a dictionary to check proper use as well as to call your attention to any errors in spelling or punctuation. The word processor can be instructed to search through a document to find a specific word or series of words in a document, making possible the quick location of a particular place to make a correction or to check a point for accuracy. It is also possible to replace a particular word or phrase wherever it occurs throughout the document. For example, every occurrence of the letters "USA" could immediately be changed throughout the document to "United States of America." Some word processors will insert footnotes properly at the bottom of the page. It is possible to produce sermons, letters, manuscripts, reports, and other documents without mistakes and corrections take little time to make.

Word processors make retyping unnecessary. Suppose, for example, that after a sermon is prepared, it is decided that the last paragraph should really be the second paragraph. Do you now get out the scissors and paste? Do you find yourself typing several versions in order to try a paragraph here or there? Good professional writing always involves a great deal of this kind of reorganization of text material.

With a word processor, the copy of the text that has been saved on the computer's disk can be called back into the computer memory at any time to make simple or drastic changes. Four or five key strokes will direct the computer to delete some phrases from one position and insert them in a new place. The sermon can then be printed out in its corrected form. The copy can be printed one time in double space and, with no more than three or four keystrokes, be printed another time with single spacing.

One pastor, who frequently sends copies of sermons to shut-ins and people who are out of town, now uses his word processor to send the sermons as personalized letters. The church office also uses the word processor to send a personalized form letter to people who attend ser-

WORK PROCESSOR   Column = 2   Row = 32

(Date)

(title) (firstnm) (lastnm)
(address)
(city) (st) (zip)

Dear (firstnm),

With a computer, printer, and word processing software, it is possible for you to produce "personalized"
letters.

Sample of Personalized Letter

vices for the first time. Each communication can be changed to make it
appropriate for different individuals without destroying the original text.
The reverse procedure is also possible; a paragraph that is to be used
over and over can be kept in storage for insertion at the proper place in
any document or letter. The computer can be keyed to insert personal
names or special messages from a list of names or paragraphs that are
typed separately into the computer memory.

Because one can store text on a disk at any stage of the process, work
can be done over several days in spite of many interruptions. When the
text has finally been completed, the computer can be instructed to organize the text for printing or for transmitting over a modem to another
computer system or for displaying on a large screen, using computer
graphics and charts, to an audience.

Sermon Preparation

"But I write out my sermon in longhand," says Pastor Skeptic. "My secretary then types it."

Word processing can save a great deal of typing time, whether a secretary types the sermon or the pastor composes at a keyboard. The computer, however, is far more than an intelligent typewriter. Because a computer can be used for keeping and arranging files of sermon subjects and illustrations, it can bring a highly significant new dimension to study and research. And it can facilitate a variety of styles of sermon preparation.

One might begin by typing an outline into the word processor. The outline could be filled in with illustrations and explanatory material, which had been placed in a computer file. To keep a computer file of sermon ideas and material requires the purchase and use of special software. But word processing software might be used when material is entered into the computer for each week's sermon.

A sermon might be prepared by bringing together ideas or segments that had been typed into a computer file as they occurred during the preceding weeks or months. Main ideas can be typed into paragraphs and stored and later recalled from a computer disk for rearrangement.

Most pastors keep card files, manila folders, or envelopes in which they collect stories and articles for future sermons. Indexes can be created from collections of articles, newspaper clippings, and book notes, and each time another item is added to the collection, the index can be updated. The computer can store author, title, and subject or key-word classifications.

A computer index can be prepared to keep track of and to locate quickly all such materials by key word. The question, for example, "Where did I read that illustration about Lazarus?" could be answered quickly by a computer search through records for the key word "Lazarus." Such a system need not be limited to books and clippings but could include any kind of material from sermons, videotapes, or journals that one might want to use for reference or illustrations.

One advantage of a computerized reference system over the traditional card file is that resources can be filed with many more cross-references. The computer can sort through the material in search of any group of words or letters desired. For example, the computer could be asked to find each time the letters "j u s t" occur together. The computer would find not only the word "just" but also "justice," "justification," and "adjust." Or the computer could be instructed to find each paragraph in which both "love" and "justice" occur.

A minister's library of personal books can also benefit from computer organization. When a book is read, notes on significant ideas can be added to the computer file. A record can also be kept of books or other resource materials that are loaned to others.

Organizing Study Materials

Using a computer to improve the quality of sermons is as important as using one to prepare letter-perfect manuscripts. A pastor's studying involves collecting, sorting, and organizing information. The King James Version of the Bible is now available on computer disks that can be used with a small computer. This makes it possible to search, sort, and compare texts.

Using an electronic concordance may not always be a feasible idea, at least with a small computer and one disk drive. It would be possible, for example, to have the computer sort through the total text of the Bible to find all occurrences of the word "Jerusalem," but this would necessitate putting several diskettes into the computer's disk drive and waiting while each word in the Bible is compared to "Jerusalem." This task could be done by computer, but it is accomplished more efficiently by looking up the word in a printed concordance.

There are, however, ways in which the study of the Bible can be enhanced with computer assistance. Some of them may even be avenues to new and richer understandings of the Scriptures. Sophisticated computer analysis of biblical vocabulary patterns and grammatical constructions will be left to theological school specialists. But every minister and Christian layperson could benefit from the study of key words. The computer can search through biblical and other texts to see how a word has been used in Scripture and interpreted by major theologians across the centuries.

Any pastor with a large library of reference books, dictionaries, lexicons, and biblical commentaries can undertake such a study. How then can a computer help? First of all, one can find study material much faster. Software that enables a pastor to prepare a concordance, tailored to his or her own special needs and interests, is available.

Second, when research has been done, it can be indexed and saved for future use in one's own electronic files. During a lifetime of sermon preparation a pastor does more extensive study than one realizes. But much of it is lost after a particular sermon is delivered. And because of personal preference and interests, a particular pastor's biblical and theological study will involve certain recurring themes. Prior to computer technology few pastors were able to preserve their research and build upon it, moving deeper into meanings and relevance each time a theme was studied. Now this can change.

There can be more coordination of personal and commercial reference materials so that much research can take place quickly and sometimes even automatically as one works. For example, when one looks up a text in an electronic Bible, the computer can provide a reminder of previous references to the passage or recommend other information that would be helpful in the study.

The computer with a modem will be able to enrich the study of the pastor who does not have a large library of reference books. When theological libraries become part of data banks, a computer will make it possible for a pastor to gain access to a greater variety and quantity of study materials than in the past.

The parish library can be organized with an electronic catalog, but its system may be different from the pastor's library system, since it will not be as oriented to preaching. It may be more important for the parish library to keep a record of when and by whom materials were used. Such a computer record can help direct future purchases, can prepare lists of missing books, or can search for materials not returned. Software is now available for organizing a parish library and card catalog, for ordering books, and for keeping track of where the books are. However, the computer's ability to enlarge a parish library for more significant study and research may be its most significant contribution to study for both pastor and laity.

Research in Computer Data Banks

A computer can be connected with the electronic catalogs of other libraries in order to sort through all computerized resources. This is evidenced by an increasing number of town libraries that have computers on which one can consult a statewide library catalog.

The day is not far off when a minister, working in the church study, will be able to access a reference catalog, like that of the Library of Congress, in computer form. It will then be possible to review most of the published material on any topic, including the latest journals, newspapers, research newsletters, and so on in just a few minutes.

Anyone with a computer and modem can now research many subjects without leaving home. The amount of information in commercial data banks is increasing every month. It will be possible to bring large amounts of material in computerized form into the church office.

A first-time user of commercial data banks is likely to be overwhelmed with all of the resources discovered. One church member on an action committee, gathering material on housing for the elderly, asked the computer at the New York State Library for a bibliography. The computer sorted through newspaper, magazine, and book review indexes and produced a hundred pages of titles. It is important, therefore, to select key words that are as explicit as possible. For example, asking for references to "love and justice" would probably provide many thousands of citations. "Tillich, love, and justice" would get more specific references.

Available Data Banks

At the present time it is possible to obtain newspaper and research journal indexes and vast amounts of practical data from computerized data banks, such as CompuServe, The Source, and NewsNet. Several commercial firms offer such services to anyone who has the proper hardware and software to connect a computer to the telephone lines and who is willing to pay to receive information. These services vary greatly in their cost and helpfulness to a church. Obtaining certain data may be more expensive than obtaining other data from the same electronic utility, depending on the source.

One pays for these services much as one pays for telephone use. For example, The Source, a subsidiary of The Reader's Digest Association, Inc., had an initial fee in 1982 of one hundred dollars. Then a subscriber paid a minimum monthly fee, much as one pays for a telephone. There is a charge for each minute that the customer is connected to the distant computer, much as the charge for a long-distance call. It can be as little as five dollars an hour at night or on weekends. During business hours the charge is about twice as much. If one's main interest in using a computer is to have a commercial data base for research, a relatively inexpensive terminal will do.

The advantages of electronic utilities over other methods of obtaining study material is that up-to-date facts can be obtained very quickly. NewsNet is an information utility that makes research newsletters available. It charges a registration fee and monthly minimum charge and hourly costs for reading. The hourly costs for one newsletter are often different from another because the fee is set by the publisher.

A special feature of NewsNet is NewsFlash, which is something like an electronic clipping service. Each subscriber can designate up to ten words or phrases that will be checked automatically against each new article, from newsletters on education, business, government, publishing, and so forth, that is added to the utility. If a match is made, the subscriber is notified the next time he or she is connected to the service. For an additional fee the NewsNet computer will dial your telephone number each time a match is made, informing you that a new item on the subject you requested is available. Such a service could be invaluable, for example, to persons who are seeking to follow the course of certain legislation through Congress, keeping them informed on the latest developments and alerting them when Congress is about to vote or conduct a hearing.

United Methodist Communications has experimented with distributing news through NewsNet. And Robert Cramer, of Resources for Communication, has published a newsletter on NewsNet including information that would be of interest to churches.

The Source offers many research services not related to sermon preparation, such as news, weather, sports reports, financial information, airline schedules, entertainment and movie reviews, computer games, and language instruction. But it also offers electronic mail services. Subscribers to The Source can communicate directly. A pastor in one city types at a computer terminal and the words appear on the screen of a colleague in a distant city. Illustrations can be sent directly and the material discussed as each person types in comments. It would be possible for a group of pastors in different cities to undertake some joint sermon preparation on a Thursday night! Because there are many places where a local phone call will connect one to The Source, direct computer communication can be less expensive than long distance telephone calls. But the major advantage is the ability to exchange documents quickly.

Robert Cramer has described how he used The Source to send, instantaneously, for forty-eight cents, a document that would have cost him ten dollars in gasoline, postage, and other charges to send through the post office. This is how he did it. He prepared the text on his word processor and called The Source on his local toll-free Tymet number, taking about a minute of time to log into the computer system. Next he typed the words "MAIL SEND," to order his computer to send electronic mail, and pushed his terminal's button labeled "RUN MESSAGE." The text in his computer's memory was converted into sound signals by the modem and these were sent over phone lines, through the central computers of The Source in McLean, Virginia, to a church in Dallas, Texas. The five-minute operation, which cost forty-eight cents at night, would have cost $1.50 during business hours.

In Dallas, the receiver simply phoned The Source, toll-free, and typed into his computer the code "MAILCK" (for "mail check") to see if there were any messages. The Source replied, "ONE UNREAD"; so he typed "MAIL SCAN" to see what it was. The computer told him the date of the message, what it contained, and who it was from. He could then request that the message be typed out on his computer's printer if he wished.[1]

In the summer of 1983 the United Methodist Church experimented with using The Source for electronic mail between agencies, conferences, and local churches.

Another electronic utility used by many church people is CompuServe, which is similar to The Source, with electronic mail service. There is an initial fee for signing up for the service, but there is no minimum monthly charge. This means that it can be used occasionally, without a commitment for extended use.

A valuable research tool for pastors is the electronic *Religion Index*[2] which since 1960 has organized data from books, monographs, journals, theses, book reviews, and so forth. It is operated by Bibliographic Retrieval Services, Inc. (BRS) and is updated monthly. Pastors who are near a seminary library can save money by using it in book form. Those who are not so located may choose the more expensive alternative of scanning abstracts of religious literature via computer screen and then ordering printouts of full articles through the BRS's AFTER DARK service. At night this service costs six dollars an hour, calculated to the nearest minute on line. The user incurs long-distance phone charges also; so this can become very expensive. Cramer suggests that regional denominational offices or audiovisual centers might consider providing such services for parish churches.

Pastors as Researchers

As people increasingly become overwhelmed with an information glut, it may become the pastor's responsibility to sort out the religious issues and data that are important for church members to have in a computer age. A parish may decide to provide computer research facilities for the pastor so that he or she can do research for community service agencies, parishioners, and others. This would be consistent with the tradition of the pastor as the person to whom the community turns for information and guidance.

The computer's potential as a research tool is illustrated by the catalog listing of information available from the Lockheed Company. It's Dialog data bank makes available information from publications of more than 400 federal government agencies. It contains more than 4,500 records of ongoing research descriptions, bibliographic references, and service program listings. A pastor might turn to Dialog for information on child abuse and other social problems.

Dialog also provides computer users with the indexes and summaries of articles from Educational Resources Informational Center (ERIC), over 400 publications in the field of education. It provides historical abstracts, information on the environment, a philosophers' index, psychological abstracts, an index to a thousand important social-science journals from all over the world, and abstracts from the natural and physical sciences.

We have mentioned only a few of the more than a thousand data banks and services available via computer, but this is enough to suggest the excellence of this new tool for pastors.

Footnotes

¹ Robert Cramer, Resources for Communications News Service, 341 Mark West Station Road, Windsor, CA 95492.
² Bibliographic Retrieval Services, 1200 Route 7, Latham, NY 12110.

For More Information

The magazine *Computers and the Humanities* reports on computer use in study and research. See Parker Rossman, "The Coming Great Electronic Encyclopedia," *The Education Digest* (December 1982); the computer magazine, *Commodore*, vol. 4, no. 5, describes a computer screen designed for presentations to large groups. See also Kenneth Bedell, "Word Processing," *Clergy Journal* (January 1983).

Checklist

Would you use a parish computer to:
—prepare sermons and other manuscripts?
—do Bible study and personal concordance preparation?
—do research from commercial data banks?

—check bibliography in libraries through computer networking?
—exchange sermon criticism and ideas with other parishes?
—index personal and parish library books and information?
—prepare files of forthcoming sermons?
—make an index of ideas, quotations, research notes?

Computers in
Church Office Work

Much of what happens in a church office involves keeping, updating, and using lists of information or data bases. Data-base management may be a parish's first use of computers. A Presbyterian survey found that three-fourths of the churches wanted to use a computer to help with data management. Sixty-five percent wanted their own computer system. They hoped to keep nominating-committee data, attendance and visitation records, financial records, stewardship records, inventories, records of individual interests and expertise, membership data, Christian education rolls, and other lists.[1]

"Some business firms are spending hundreds of thousands of dollars on electronic office equipment," says Pastor Hopeful. "Can we at least get rid of our old addressograph machine?"

Mailing Lists

Any list can be placed in a computer. Many churches will think first of computerizing their mailing lists. Once a mailing list has been saved on a disk, it is available not only to produce mailing labels but also to be updated, sorted, and printed out in various ways. A mailing list can be kept accurate more easily with a computer than by most other methods. The computer list saves money, and the church benefits from the reduction of embarrassing mistakes.

Computerization of the mailing list will produce some changes in the way office work is organized and will yield the most benefit when one master list of all names and addresses is created. Most churches now have many separate lists, such as lists of people who receive mailings for the church school, the women's group, the men's group, or the trustees. Sometimes these lists are kept by different people. When all information is kept together on one computerized list, one correction or change of address is made automatically in all lists.

The master list can be coded (for example, participant in youth group, nonmember soloist, possible interest in Bible study group) so that many different kinds of sublists can be produced from it. Often the mailing list is kept in zip code order for postal convenience of parish mailings. But with a computer one can sort the list in other ways. One could obtain an alphabetical (names or addresses) list, a list of people living on a particular street, or a list of senior citizens living in one part of town. The computer makes it possible to use the mailing list in many new ways that were difficult before computerization.

Data-Base Management

Data-base management software can be purchased for almost all computer equipment sold today. Available software varies a great deal in ease of use, the number of items that can be included in a list, the amount of information that can be stored about each item, ability to manipulate information, speed of reorganizing and updating lists, and cost. Most parishes will want to find a data-base management software package that will do at least the following things:

—define what information will be stored in each list.
—enter and update lists.
—search through a list to find a particular word, number, or group of letters.
—put a list in an order that is different from that in which it was entered.
—produce reports by reordering, sorting, selecting, counting, or adding information.
—prepare and print out a church directory.

Some data-base management software packages have additional features. Some will print out mailing labels or save a report on a disk in such a way that it can be used by a word-processing program in personalized letters. Others include security precautions so that only certain people will be able to access or change the lists.

When first setting up a data-base management system, it is usually necessary to decide what and how much data is to be stored about each item. Each parish needs to decide which of its lists will benefit from computerization. It is usually not a wise use of a computer to store information that will not be processed.

A side comment: Computers should rarely be used simply for storage. Printed copies of important information should always be made and kept in a safe place since a computer system is vulnerable to mechanical failure. Time generally should not be spent typing into a computer old church records that will not be updated and that can be consulted easily in printed form. If historical information should be needed in the computer for use in comparison with current data in a long-range study, it can be added at the time the study is made.

With some software it is easy to change the initial parameters if it is later decided that different information would be more useful. But there are data-base management software packages which demand that all decisions about what information will be saved be made when the computer system is first set up. Such church software programs come with the data base already defined.

In any case, it can take from a few minutes to many hours to set up a data base, depending on the knowledge of the person setting it up, the sophistication of the data-base software, and the nature of the tasks which the software will be asked to do. So a parish may want to begin collecting and organizing needed information even before a computer is secured. After the data base has been set up, the users only enter and update information and generate reports from the information.

Some data-base management software packages can be used with a number of different lists. The same one might be used, for example, for the mailing list and the inventory of choir music. Some data-base management programs make it possible for the computer system to use information from several lists at once. For example, membership records might be on one list and members' contributions on another. To get a list of people who have been members for more than five years who contribute less than two dollars a week, it would be necessary to have a data-base software package that could use both lists simultaneously.

Word Processing

Word processing can help the church office prepare all kinds of documents, reports, and letters with more speed and efficiency than in the past. If similar letters are to be sent to several people, the basic copy needs to be typed into the computer but once, and each letter can be personalized, with the computer inserting different information for each person as that letter is printed out. The time saved in preparing person-

Time Saved by Use of Computer in the Church Office

The initial data collection and entry process needed to set up the system is quite time consuming. However, after the system has been set up, maintaining the records involves a very small amount of time and can often be done by volunteers. This chart* shows the time saved in one 850-member church using a computer to do the following functions.

Function	Previous Time	Computer Time
Giving Records		
Recording individual amounts	4 hours	2.5 hours
Posting to individual pledge records	3 hours	20 seconds
Posting to individual giving records	3 hours	20 seconds
Preparing individual giving statements	8-10 hours	30-40 minutes
Preparing detailed giving statements	40-60 hours	1.5 hours
Bookkeeping (time per month)		
Entering receipts and expenditures	20-25 hours	6-8 hours
Posting to general ledger	10-15 hours	3 minutes
Posting to payroll ledger	3-4 hours	2 minutes
Posting to budget return ledger	3 hours	5 minutes
Preparing and printing itemized budget report showing expenditures and balances, current period and year-to-date	15-20 hours	10 minutes
Preparing and printing financial statements	1.5 hours	4 minutes
Membership Records		
Registering weekly attendance	4 hours	2 hours
Preparing and printing up-to-date membership lists (names, addresses, family members, work and home telephone numbers)	15-20 hours	30 minutes

*From John Wesley United Methodist Church, Tallahassee, Florida alized form letters, such as those sent to another congregation about a transfer of membership or a request for date of baptism, can be substantial. All such routine correspondence can be handled this way, using forms kept on a computer disk.

Using a word processor to replace the typewriter makes the production of worship bulletins, newsletters, meeting notices, and minutes much more efficient and pleasant. In preparing a worship bulletin, for example, the standard order of worship generally does not change from week to week. The previous week's bulletin can be brought onto the screen from the computer's memory, and one can quickly change hymn numbers, prayers, Scripture readings, sermon titles, and announcements without having to retype the entire bulletin. If the church uses a mimeograph, a computer printer that will type stencils should be purchased. (Ink jet and some of the more expensive letter-quality printers will not type stencils.) After the bulletin is prepared and corrected on the word processor, the computer will print out an error-free stencil.

Information for a church bulletin or newsletter can be typed into the computer whenever a notice is received, even weeks in advance, and be kept on the computer disk until needed. When a word processor is used, the items on the disk can be edited and rearranged on the day the newsletter is prepared for publication.

A bulletin or newsletter can be printed out first onto a plain piece of paper so that the layout can be checked before the bulletin is printed onto a stencil. Many computer printers will produce photo-ready copy, which does not need to be reset, for offset printing. All computer printers produce copy that can be used for dry copy reproduction. If a newsletter is printed by a commercial company, the type can in some cases be sent directly from the church office to the printing plant, computer to computer, by telephone. A company in California, for example, receives material from all over the country through the CompuServe computer electronic utility and returns photo-ready type through the mail. A company in Virginia has a toll-free telephone number which can be called to send text directly to their typesetting facility.

Talents of Members

In smaller congregations, the pastor or other leaders will be familiar with the gifts and talents of most of the members. But even in a medium-sized parish it becomes difficult to match well the talents and interests of people with jobs and responsibilities. In a larger church it has been almost impossible to avoid overlooking many people. With a computer it is possible not only to keep track of the answers people give on questionnaires about their interests and talents, but also to keep and use comprehensive records of people's past service and participation.

Computerization solves the major problems that parish leaders usually face in trying to set up a talent bank. If a talent bank is organized on file cards with each person's name at the top and interests written below, it is difficult to find a piano player without reading through all of the cards. If each talent is given a separate card with names written on it, then it is very difficult to keep the file updated as people move away or change their interests. Trying to keep an adequately cross-referenced card file is not impossible but is very difficult.

With a computer, cross-referencing is very simple. Once the information has been entered into the computer, it can be printed out in any form desired. One time it might be helpful to have a list of all the piano players. Another time one might need to know the piano players who can also provide transportation. In another situation, one might want to determine the talents of a particular person. Updating the talent bank is done easily with a computer. If it is discovered that although six people indicated an interest in scout work, none will actually help with a troop, the category can easily be removed.

Some churches might find it useful to keep additional information in the computer talent file, information such as when a person was last asked to help or to use a talent and how a talent was used. If proper information is added to the talent file, the file can be used to compile an annual report of members' participation, to prepare a study of inactive members, to analyze the extent to which people have been asked to do what they are willing to do, or to discover which people are being underused. But it takes time to keep a talent file updated with this information. A church must decide whether the information from these reports is worth the constant effort of updating files.

Inventories

A computer is ideally suited to the task of keeping inventories. Some insurance companies demand that there be current inventories of all movable property owned by the parish. Computerized inventories can be more easily prepared, updated, and reorganized than inventories kept on a piece of paper. Much less time is needed in deciding when, where, and what to order when new supplies are needed. For example, a computer inventory of church music can record titles, composers, number of copies, and dates used. One can easily discover whether the church has copies of certain music, and one can analyze the use of particular music. Computerization of the music inventory is more useful than a card file system, because the computer can sort through the records to find a particular piece of music by any of the characteristics that are stored in the inventory. The computer could find all compositions of Bach, could tell one what music was used by the choir on the previous Easter, or could list all the pieces in the church collection for which the church has more than forty copies.

Inventories of religious-education resources can benefit similarly from computerization. The church office's inventories might include a record of who has used the resource in the past so that a church school teacher can talk to the person in the parish who is the most familiar with a particular resource. A computerized inventory of materials can be analyzed to discover what resources are available for each age group. Rarely used materials can be pinpointed for evaluation to see if they should be kept. But the major benefit of computerization of all church materials, resources, and equipment is to help the church office make them more accessible to the people who need them. The question "What do we have on Romans to help with my fourth-grade church school class?" can be quickly and accurately answered.

Financial Records

A computer is ideally suited to improve the quality and efficiency of church financial records and reports. Weekly contributions must be accurately recorded, and monthly and quarterly reports sent to contributors. Treasurers' reports with monthly and quarterly receipts and expenditures must also be prepared in such a way that an officer or committee member can know how much remains to be spent on a particular budget item. In many parishes, contributions may be made regularly to a number of separate funds. Statements of each fund must be made available when needed for inclusion in regular monthly, quarterly, and annual financial reports.

There may still be church treasurers who prefer to record all church finances by hand. But when a parish computerizes all of its financial records, any committee or officer can have an immediately updated report on a particular fund, on a budget item, or on the status of the entire budget without waiting for the production of a monthly or quarterly report. The computer can also analyze giving patterns to identify, for example, categories of people who give more than they did in previous years or those who gave more than $600 last year but are currently giving much less. The results of such analyses can be used in budget planning and for stewardship projects.

The most beneficial software for recording church contributions will accept data in a clear, simple form. Usually this means that only an envelope number and amount need to be entered. The computer can then credit the correct contributor. It should also be possible to enter a code for a particular fund or designation with each contribution. If an envelope number is not known, but only the contributor's name, it should be possible to enter the name and amount and have the computer find the correct record and credit the contributor. This software should also provide for an easy way to add a new contributor.

It should be unnecessary to enter financial information more than once. A computer can be programmed to post the entry to the proper accounts and credit it where necessary. A list of each week's contributions and current account balances should also be kept in printed form in case of computer failure. A computer may only slightly reduce the time needed to post contributions each week, but it will save much time in the production of reports. Once report formats are set up using the data-base management software, widely varying reports can at any time be produced and printed out with very little human effort.

Bookkeeping

A church treasurer can use a computer much as an accountant uses a computer in business for bookkeeping and accounting. Bookkeeping software for churches is available, but software designed for small businesses could also be used by a parish. Most congregations use general-ledger and accounts-payable programs. A separate payroll software package may be helpful for parishes that have several employees.

Computerized bookkeeping systems function on the same principles as manual systems but with two major differences. Entries, made only once, may be posted in several places. And reports may be generated quickly. A computer has several other advantages. It is very good at adding a long column of figures. Each entry can be given several category identifiers so that it is possible to analyze how money is being spent by a parish; for example, expenditures might normally be reported in broad budget categories, such as supplies, maintainance, salaries. This method allows easy comparisions of expenditures and budget. And planning is facilitated if expenditures to date are reported by program categories. The computer can quickly prepare either kind of report if each expenditure is coded for the program area to which it is related.

Expenditures such as the electric bill can be divided and charged to various program categories.

The ease in generating reports facilitates control of church expenditures. A decision about whether to purchase equipment for the church school can be based on current information about expenditures, rather than on a treasurer's monthly report that might not include bills paid within recent weeks.

Calendar of Minister and Church

When one has a printed calendar, it is necessary to look at each entry when the date of a particular meeting has been forgotten. A computerized calendar will do this searching quickly and efficiently. If a meeting is scheduled on the third Tuesday of every month, the computer can automatically insert the entry for months in advance. Computerized calendars are very easy to update and can be very comprehensive, including as many community or denominational meeting dates as may be desired. Daily, weekly, or monthly schedules can be printed out so that there is an easy-to-read reminder of commitments. The computer can list all commitments in order and signal any conflicts.

This record of dates, times, and commitments, along with a computerized record of the number of hours spent on administrative work, denominational responsibilities, pastoral visitation, and other activities, can be used by the computer to prepare annual reports. If the calendar data base is expanded to include all information about how time is spent, the data base can be used for more sophisticated time use and job analyses.

Project Management

Commercial software for project management needs information about the time necessary to accomplish each part of a project and the tasks that must be accomplished first. The computer uses this information to propose a schedule for the whole project, suggesting when each task must be finished in order to complete the project on time. A minister can use similar software to help with the organization of church work. Or the computer could be used by the stewardship committee to set dates and to propose what should be done each day in order to complete a financial campaign by a certain date. Or if the computer has been provided with all scheduling information for the week, it could propose which tasks must be done each day in light of special events or emergencies; for example, it could note that sermon and bulletin preparation must be started two days earlier than usual because of scheduled weddings and funerals.

"Do you mean a computer is going to tell me what to do?" Pastor Skeptic interrupts.

Certainly not. The computer would only make proposals and give reminders. On the basis of information received about tasks that need to be done, the computer would organize a proposed schedule according to a predetermined plan. As a result, better organization could be brought into hectic schedules. The minister could more easily review the week's schedule in terms of long-term needs. He or she could thus better set priorities for a week or month. The computer could not make judgments about what tasks are more important, but it could help to clarify the demands that are being made and allow for rational decisions about which tasks will be given priority.

Church Office as Resource Center

The church office is a place not only where organizational work is done but also where information is kept. Because computers can transmit information quickly and computerized records take up very little space, the use of computers can lead to new thoughts about the nature of the church office. As Alvin Toffler in *The Third Wave* observes, it is no longer necessary for employees to gather in offices around filing cabinets and copy machines. A computer work station can be located at home and be connected by telephone with other work stations, thus decentralizing the office work of the church. Parish staff members working in their homes would consider their computers as the church office. They could prepare a church mailing at home, instructing the printer in the church office to print address labels.

Until now it has been necessary for many organizational tasks to be done at the office because that was where the information and equipment was. But if tomorrow most of the church data bases are stored on a computer and can be accessed through the phone lines by home computers, then much work can be done at home by pastors, church secretaries, and volunteers.

It would be possible for any church school teacher to use a home computer as a terminal for consulting materials in the parish office or library. The treasurer, working at home, can use the office computer to prepare financial reports. Other officers can use home terminals to consult minutes or to prepare an agenda. If the chairperson of the trustees wishes to know when the church roof was last repaired, the computer can sort through minutes for this information much more quickly than a person can read through files of minutes. Minutes stored on a computer could be especially helpful when several committees have worked on the same project; important items of information and decisions may be recorded in the minutes of several different groups.

As more and more homes are equipped with terminals to communicate over telephone lines to other computers, churches may want to use electronic mail systems with the church office computer as the center for sending messages between members. Although electronic mail is useful only when people check regularly for messages, a church computer can be used as a community bulletin board for announcements and as a place where members can leave messages or ask questions. Several parishes have experimented with making general announcements available on electronic bulletin boards, using the church telephone at night when the office is closed. The office phone is connected to a computer which can then answer the telephone and communicate with a member's computer.

Footnotes

[1] The Presbyterian survey of computer use, and a supplementary survey on how church people feel about computers, was conducted by The Presbyterian Panel, 1908 Interchurch Center, 475 Riverside Drive, New York, NY 10115-0099. Fifty-one percent of 748 reporting congregations said that they wished to maintain a larger variety and number of records in the future.

For More Information

The World Future Society, 4916 St. Elmo Avenue, Bethesda, MD 20814-5089, offers audiotapes on "The Emerging Electronic Office," "Telecommunity and Decentralization of the Workplace," and "Information Technology and the Organization, Social, Psychological, and Managerial Implications."

Checklist

Would your congregation use a computer to:

—istore and sort lists of new members, baptisms, funerals, weddings, attendance, and other records?

—prepare a church directory and keep a comprehensive mailing list?

—do word processing in the church office for preparing letters, documents, minutes, worship bulletins, newsletters, and other similar jobs?

—keep financial records and make reports?

—keep more comprehensive lists with more detailed data than you now do?

—keep track of and inventory all church materials and equipment?

4

Computers in Planning and Administration

Computers have the potential for radically changing the church's approach to planning and administration. Administration includes clarifying goals, identifying resources, planning and strategizing, exercising control and supervision, and evaluating. Computers can help with these activities. Church administration also includes the cultivation of leadership within the congregation and the development of organization. A congregation has no way of knowing, however, whether particular programs or strategies will actually fulfill its goals or the central purposes of the church. A parish has usually only been able to try things out in order to see what will happen. Computers may change this.

A computer can be used to project possible consequences of taking certain actions. It can analyze whether there is consistency between the nature of the church, its purpose, and its strategies. Such assessment requires that church planning begin with a statement of the nature of the church, what it is, and how it functions, that is, a model. Then a purpose statement, goals, and strategies consistent with the model need to be written. A computer model makes it possible to predict the effect of various strategies.

Using models is not new for the church. All church members, whether they realize it or not, use a mental image or model of the church in making decisions. It is impossible to avoid using this model; the only question is whether people are conscious of it and its implications. Church members need more biblically based models of the church to replace fuzzy secular models. People in a congregation often misunderstand one another, and tensions develop because they are using different models of the church without realizing it.

Computer Models of a Parish

Some thought has been given to developing computer models of the way churches function. Marvin Mickle, an engineering professor at Carnegie Mellon University, brought a computer model of a congregation, for use in parish evaluation and planning, to a 1982 conference at Pittsburgh on church use of computers. The model focused too little on spiritual nurture and too much on a congregation's performance as measured by attendance and finance. Parish use of the model, however, has helped leaders to realize the extent to which they actually use unexamined and inadequate models in their decision making.

In the future there may be computerized models for churches to use in making projections of the probable effect of certain actions, but we cannot imagine how computers could ever be able to tell a particular congregation what it should do. However, computer models can help a congregation in two ways.

First, models can aid in making predictions. Information about a congregation, its community, and larger social factors can be fed into a computer along with the parish's model, and the computer can make a prediction based on this data. But experience with incorrect computerized weather predictions in planning a picnic points to a needed caution in using computer predictions in the congregation's decision-making process.

Second, the process of model development forces a congregation to continue examining its program and its self-understanding and to modify its goals and procedures accordingly. Even if the congregation does not computerize a model of itself, a computer can help provide information to use in testing the model created by the data about the church. For example, a model of the church might include the idea that worship attendance will increase if the church school is strengthened. The computer could be used to compare church school and worship attendance during the past twenty-five years to see if the model is consistent with the facts. A congregation does not need to wait for experts to develop complicated computer models of a parish before benefiting from this new science. A computer can be used to test and examine specific parts of the existing mental model.

Suppose that the stewardship chairperson discovers that a majority of her committee feels that the parish has trouble paying its bills because not enough new people are joining the congregation, thus bringing in more money; that if the evanglism committee's work was better done, there would be no financial problems. This idea reveals a mental model of the way a parish works. The chairperson might challenge the committee to use the computer to examine this model. The number of new families joining the church might be compared with changes in parish income. The first- and second-year giving of new families might be reviewed to discover the average income that could be expected from new members. The long-term effect of involving new families in parish programs and leadership could be examined. The giving patterns of people who joined the church five, ten, and fifteen years ago could be detailed. Such factors could be laid out for study using data-base software described in the previous chapter.

If analysis of this information indicates a relationship between parish income and reception of members, the committee will want to share its findings with the evangelism committee. But the computer research may reveal that the stewardship committee must rethink its previous belief. For example, it might reveal that new members are attracted when those who already belong increase their giving.

A computer model developed by a parish must be very simple because of the difficulty of using presently available software and computer languages. Many parishes have members who can write computer programs and could prepare the software necessary to accomplish the task just described. In the future there will be church administration software designed for people without technical sophistication. The software will probably ask the user a series of questions about what a committee wishes to know. On the basis of that information, it will set up the appropriate calculations to make projections or to suggest implications.

No software was yet available for church use in 1983 comparable to CIVITEX, the Civic Information and Techniques Exchange of the National Municipal League's Citizens Forum on Self-Government. This computer data base consists of several thousand profiles (how-to-do-it illustrations or models) of community projects that can be searched for, using keywords that indicate method of process. It is intended to stimulate cross-pollination among planners and problem solvers in different communities. Some parishes are using CIVITEX for ideas to solve community problems.

Computer Simulations

Another way in which a computer can be used to discover in advance how a particular program or administrative plan may work is through simulations. A congregation may use existing software or create new simulations for itself.

"But simulations are games for youth groups," complains Pastor Skeptic. "And the simulation at our last youth retreat took about six hours. Adult committees will not be willing to spend time like that to discover the consequences of proposed actions." Computers can quickly review the reactions and responses of people.

Church use of simulations has been studied by Ellis Larsen at Wesley Theological Seminary. He gives one illustration of a simulation called the District Superintendent Game, wherein people compare the characteristics of specific Methodist congregations with information about the backgrounds and gifts of ministers who might be assigned to congregations. This simulation has been very useful in helping people understand placement issues.

The District Superintendent Game can be played without computer assistance, but the computer makes the calculations more quickly. Larsen has experimented with a finance-planning simulation that demonstrates the value of computer simulations. If financial goals and statistics are entered into a computer, the results of a strategy can be simulated in a few minutes compared to a manual calculation time of several hours.

After a simulation, the computer can predict results as they relate to church goals and values. Computer simulations can be used in the church to help people understand the possible effects of administrative decisions and procedures and to sensitize members to issues in the interrelationship of people and groups.

Spread Sheets

Computerizing spread sheets can be a great help in parish administration, making it possible to enter financial information and calculate totals and averages so that the data can be used for more effective budget evaluation and planning.

Most church treasurers record expenditures on a spread sheet, a large page with columns labeled for each budget category. Each expenditure is entered as a line with the check number in one column, possibly a brief explanation in another column, and the amount in the column under the budget category. At the end of the month the columns are added to find the total spent in each budget category and these are added across to calculate the total spent. With computer software such figures can be changed and rearranged on a screen with astonishing ease.

Spread-sheet software can also be used to help prepare the budget. In planning future budgets, the first column might contain the budget for each item, the second column the subcategory; the third would have last year's expenditure for the item; and the fourth would report this year's expenditure to date. The fifth could suggest a budget amount for next year from the appropriate program committee. The computer can reorganize and manipulate the information in many different ways. Additional columns could be calculated and filled in, such as a sixth column that might project this year's expenditures at the end of the year on the basis of data in column four.

A finance committee could use the computer spread-sheet software to calculate the answers to "what if" questions. For example, what if energy costs were increased 10 percent, requests of the program groups were funded in full, salaries were increased 4 percent, and mission giving was increased 20 percent? The computer would calculate each line item, add up subtotals for categories, and provide a figure for the total budget. Spread-sheet software could also put a star in each column where the item is running 20 percent above last year's spending. The computer could also calculate the percentage of the proposed budget going to various categories. These could be compared by the computer to percentages calculated from previous years to give an idea of the changing priorities reflected in certain budget proposals.

Church schools often use a spread sheet to record attendance. A paper is divided into columns, with each church school class given one column. A line is used for each Sunday's attendance. The date is written in the first column, attendance at each class is recorded in the proper columns, and the total attendance for the Sunday is given in the final column. With computer software, the average attendance for each class can be calculated by adding the column for that class and dividing the total by the number of Sundays.

Spread-sheet software varies a great deal in its ability to manipulate numbers and to generate reports, in the amount of information with which it can work, and in its ease of use. Some spread-sheet software provides little more than a way to type columns of numbers onto a computer screen and to use the computer to add the total. Others limit the number of columns of information that can be used at one time or the number of entries possible for each column. With some spread-sheet software, it is possible to move information from the data-base management or word-processing programs into the spread-sheet program. This may be important if the spread sheet will be used with information that is collected for another purpose.

Computers and Meetings

Using a computer to store and organize information can greatly reduce the number of times when a chairperson must say, "I'll need to look that up and bring the answer to the next meeting." Church administration can be facilitated when questions of fact can be answered promptly and when calculations can be made even while a meeting is in progress.

The parish with a computer can experiment with new styles of administration. For example, oral or printed reports need no longer be prepared before a meeting. The computer's ability to generate reports and analyze statistics quickly can make it possible for those responsible for an agenda to define at the beginning of a meeting what information will be needed and in what form. The computer can then generate the desired reports, including the most up-to-date data, as the meeting begins.

Some parishes may want to experiment with telemeetings. Without gathering at a specific time or place, members of a committee may receive reports, raise questions, interact with each other, and even vote on motions, using computer terminals in their homes. Such computer conferencing is now extensively used in education and industry. A computerized bulletin board can be used to inform or poll members to involve the whole congregation when emergency decisions need to be made. The face-to-face value of Christian interaction, however, is such that most congregations are far from planning to use computers in such avant-garde ways.

Computers and Organization

Many of the obvious uses of a computer for handling details in the organizational life of a parish are not discussed here, because they are described in other chapters. The possibilities for keeping track of all the meetings, the people involved, their leadership training, and so on, depend upon the software used in the parish.

MIST is being used by a church in San Francisco.[1] It is designed to make it easy for amateurs to do word processing, data-base management, and telecommunications. MIST can help people with common interests get in touch with each other. MIST's keyword, interactive retrieval, and flexible list and report capabilities are ideal for preparing keyword searches, indexes, skill or talent banks, and community memories. It can simplify and automate the often complicated connect routines of the electronic utilities and commercial data bases. A MIST user can simply type in the name of the system to which he or she wishes to connect, and MIST handles all of the complex procedures. A user can send or receive messages with a single command. MIST has also been used for simultaneous linking of computers at different conferences.

Footnotes

[1] MIST is available from New Era Technologies, 2025 Eye Street, N.W., Washington, DC 20006.

For More Information

See Jeffrey Rothfeder, "A Congregational Computation," *Personal Computing* (April 1983), which reports that a parish in Houston has spent $100,000 on a highly sophisticated computer system. For information about the Citizens Forum on Self Government, phone 800-223-6004. *Resources for Communication* (Sept. 12, 1983), reports the need for new types of software to integrate various programs for file management.

Check List

Would your congregation use a computer to:
—make projections for budget planning using computer spread sheets?
—create simulations or do research for other kinds of administration and planning to discover potential implications or consequences of planned programs?
—develop models, purposes, goals, objectives, and strategies for evaluation?
—handle administrative detail, such as scheduling of meetings, sending reminders, preparing agendas?
—experiment with new styles of administration, computer conferencing, and so on?
—use a software spread sheet for annual program planning?
—keep minutes and reports in such a form that they could be used during meetings?

Computer Modeling

A computer model is a set of rules about the way certain events or situations interact. These rules are programmed into a computer so that, manipulating large amounts of data very quickly, it can receive information about a situation and calculate projections.

M.I.T. Professor Jay Forrester used system dynamics in preparing a computer model for community development, which could predict, among other things, the impact on employment of city investment in low-income housing. A group of computer and social scientists, the Club of Rome, used computers to project the impact of unchecked population growth by the year 2100.

Such uses of computers require the development of clear and accurate models. M.I.T. Professor Joseph Weizenbaum believes that it will be impossible to develop models that are sophisticated enough for social planning. On the other hand, economist Hazel Henderson is far more optimistic about the use of computer models to make values decisions and to solve some of society's problems.

Computers in Evangelism and Mission

Computers and evangelism?" Pastor Skeptic shook his head. "No electronic machine can replace the human being as a witness to Christ's gospel."

Of course not! But computers can process information and that can be especially helpful in outreach and evangelism. Computers, like telephones that extend our voices and automobiles that extend our legs, are instruments we can use for good or ill. They can help us to organize what we know about people so that we can make better use of the information. They can help us to coordinate information in useful ways for presentations. And they can aid with the preparation of presentations of the gospel. Presenting the gospel, after all, is processing and communicating information.

So computers can profoundly affect church growth, evangelism, and mission. Computers can help the church in remarkable ways if church people are clear about what they want to do and how they are going to do it. Without reducing evangelism and outreach to techniques, we can be good stewards of electronic tools in the service of Christ and the gospel.

Evangelism and mission begin with three rather simple goals: finding people, reaching out to cultivate and keep in touch with people, and winning people to decision and church membership.

Finding People

American churches have had an easy time for much of this century. New members have come easily. Christians have not had to go out into the highways and byways, as Jesus taught, to look for the lost sheep. Churches have for the most part been content with the ninety and nine. Much evangelism has been directed toward recruiting already committed persons to membership. Even radio and TV preaching, intended for nonchurch people, has tended to reach only those who are already committed.

Yet the task of evangelism requires finding and winning those who have no significant commitment to Jesus Christ, as well as finding and involving those who have some commitment but are not involved in the life of a congregation. First they must be found, and that is a crucially important task in which computers can be helpful.

Most churches, even those that say they have few prospective members, have a great deal of unused information, like large sums of money in the bank they don't know how to get or use. For example, many uncommitted persons at one time attended Sunday church school or a youth group. They were lost from sight because the task of keeping track of everyone who once attended was too large for the congregation to handle. A careful survey of church membership and attendance records would discover many prospective members related in some way to church families. The grown child who has an apartment of her own yet does not receive church mailings because she is still included with her parents on the church address list is one type of person easily lost.

One church began to make a note of every new person who contacted the church for some reason. After several months the church realized that many nonchurch persons were, in fact, in touch with the church occasionally. These people were all potential new members, but for years no one had been keeping track of them or initiating further involvement.

In search of new prospects, many congregations conduct a house-by-house survey of the neighborhood, use federal census information, or send out questionnaires to members about neighbors, friends, and workplace acquaintances. If such research into the community is done well, church leaders are overwhelmed by more information than they can ever correlate or use effectively without a vast staff or computers.

"We have a lot of that data on cards stored in the church attic," says Pastor Hopeful. "Some of it is completely useless, coming from surveys ten to thirty years ago. It was used at the time to make a list of prospective members. Then I guess people forgot about it or did not know how else to use it. There was just too much of it!"

Unless a congregation has a good deal of money to spend on research

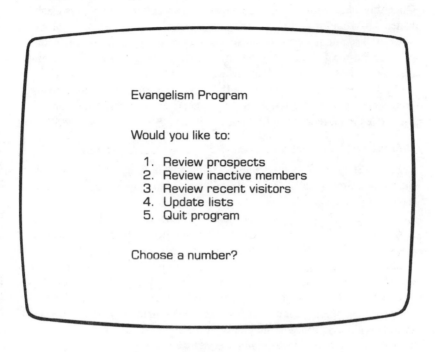

Evangelism Program

Would you like to:

1. Review prospects
2. Review inactive members
3. Review recent visitors
4. Update lists
5. Quit program

Choose a number?

Sample of "Menu" for Evangelism Program

or has a corps of lay members with computers, much of this old survey information should not be placed in a computer data bank. In most cases the time and energy spent typing in the old data could be better spent collecting and entering current survey results, although it might sometimes be helpful to compare old and new surveys to see how the neighborhood has changed. Do new residents tend to be significantly different in terms of age, ethnic heritage, or religious persuasion?

Most software packages designed for churches sort and organize survey information. Thus a thorough, community survey will be necessary to take full advantage of the computer. Members of the congregation may be more enthusiastic to do the work once they learn that computer sorting and organization of the data will make possible much more use of the data now and for a long time in the future. A computer can sort out information about people surveyed by the respondent's age, sex, place of work, special interests and needs, and past religious affiliations. Once this data bank of information about prospective members is established, information can be added easily.

Churches might eventually use computers to keep a file on every person within a few miles of the church, thus taking seriously the commission of Jesus to go out into the world and seek out *all persons.*

While a computer will not actually find prospects for a church, using a computer makes it possible to keep better track of prospects and to use surveys and records to find them.

Outreach and Cultivation

Pastor Skeptic says, however, "I already know about more people than I have time to call on and I already know more about their problems than I can deal with."

If it is true that Pastor Skeptic already has more information about unreached people in the community than can be used, then obviously a computer will be most useful if it can carry some of this burden. Some churches are finding that a computer can help to mobilize and organize the work of many more members who help with programs. Everyone knows that astonishing things can be accomplished if large numbers of people give even modest sums of money and contribute modest amounts of time regularly. But without a computer, an organizational genius and a great amount of administrative time are needed to keep a system going in which every person carries a fair share of the load.

One way a computer can help is to keep track of the best person to do each job. People become irritated if they are repeatedly asked to do things which they cannot or will not do and are never asked to serve in ways for which they have expressed willingness to serve.

While computer use in church work should be a matter of biblical stewardship and not mere business efficiency, a bit of efficiency, nevertheless, can help contribute to high standards of excellence and to good public relations in outreach. A computer does not forget, as human beings do. It does not get tired of reminding people again and again.

A computer can manage a system in which every member is reminded to contact one new person each week. It can supply that member with helpful information about the needs and interests of the new person, of present and past church involvements, and of items of interest to the person contacted. Instead of the caller phoning to say, "We hope you will come to church Sunday" (which may sound like nagging), the caller can be helped to say, "I understand you are interested in sports; so I thought you might be interested in knowing that the sermon next Sunday will be about the testimony of a well-known athlete.''

Some people fear that computers will bring a depersonalizing trend to the church, but the fact is that a computer can help make outreach much more personal. Most of the commercial software available in 1984 for use in churches is specifically designed to make lists of people with common interests. This can be used, therefore, not only to match up callers with new people with similar interests, but also to implement some significant kinds of outreach that most congregations have found difficult to undertake.

Specific programs tailored to involve special groups of people can be planned when detailed information about people's interests is known. Leaders of one congregation, for example, assumed that many of the unmarried young people who lived in converted old houses near the church were not interested in church attendance. The computer processing of more adequate information about them showed that there were many different types of young people there who should be treated as individuals and not all be lumped together in a disinterested category.

When properly approached, some of these young people helped conduct and computerize a survey of unemployed people in the area. When they found a need for a food kitchen, these previously unchurched young couples turned out to be the most dependable help when it came to scrubbing the floors, washing the dishes, and doing the other hard work that made it possible for the congregation to serve this need. Many of them eventually joined the church. Although uninterested in attending the sort of activities that older people had planned, they were interested in planning and attending their own kinds of Bible study and prayer exploration groups.

Winning People

"So computers can be of great help to congregations in finding prospective members and in organizing information with which to reach out and cultivate their interest more effectively," says Pastor Hopeful. "But how can computers help in the more difficult and sensitive work of moving people to decision, to church membership, to deep commitment?"

Many churches use computers to help them organize traditional evangelistic programs. Suppose, for example, a congregation is planning a revival campaign or preaching mission. Computerized word processing can be used to prepare publicity. The church's data base can be used to match callers with prospects. A computerized spread sheet can help with financial planning. Computerization of results will help to organize follow-up.

If a congregation is planning a program of visitation to talk to people about making a commitment, computers can prepare lists and match prospects with callers. Church members can be trained through Computer Assisted Instruction, which is discussed in the next chapter. Much more information about the person being visited can be provided to the caller when the church's data base is computerized. Pierre Babin has suggested that Christians cannot effectively evangelize until they are "really present" in the world they are addressing and until they engage people in a two-way communication that involves deep levels of meaning. This is possible when a computer helps to sort out more information on people's needs, interests, and problems.

Computers can also help in the development of new and alternative forms of evangelism that may be more effective with people who are not responding to present programs. Some people who are not reached by evangelistic preaching will respond in face-to-face groups in which the gospel can be seen, felt, and understood emotionally as well as intellectually. Computers can make it possible for people to be invited to the right kinds of groups and for the churches to know what kinds of groups should be formed. Caring groups can be created with more facility with the help of computers. In the United States today there are more than seven hundred thousand groups that meet regularly to help members deal with special problems. Alcoholics Anonymous was one of the first. Such face-to-face groups have, in many cases, become highly effective instruments of evangelism with people who have not responded to traditional approaches.

Caring groups can be created without the help of computers. Churches do it all the time. A notice can be placed in the newspaper and on bulletin boards, for example, inviting all parents of children who have cancer to come to the church on Wednesday night. But to find or create groups for all of the different kinds of crises and problems that people have is generally found to be too complex and time-consuming a task without computer help.

A computer can also help to develop vocational evangelism. Any pastor knows that it is often the school teacher who invites and brings a new teacher to church. It is likely to be a factory worker who invites a new employee from work. How, though, can the factory worker play a more constructive role in decision making and commitment? Often group meetings are the situation in which commitments are explored. In vocational evangelism this exploration is done in the context of the relation of the Christian faith to one's work. Christian businessmen have lunch meetings; nurses meet for Bible study at a hospital; or politicians get together for a prayer breakfast.

The effectiveness of groups of Christians meeting by vocation is well known but has not often been implemented because of the difficulty of matching people by vocation and interest. A computer can sort and match members and prospects by vocation and place of work.

Not only can computers help with organizing traditional evangelistic programs and with developing helping groups for faith development and vocational evangelism programs, but computers can also assist with the preparation of evangelistic messages that are sent over the public media.

Effective Use of Electronic Media

The telephone, radio, and TV are all electronic media that churches can use today. In the near future, teletext and videotex will also be available. Each of these forms of communication can be used more effectively for evangelism with computers.

As more church members have computer terminals in their homes, it will be possible to use the church computer to communicate with these members by means of their home computers. A church with a computer message system can have the computer answer the telephone in the evening. The computer can give messages, provide a bulletin board, or take a message from church members calling in. A Methodist minister has set up such a system for a computer newsletter he edits. When he can't answer the phone, the computer still receives messages from or gives messages to anyone who calls and has a home terminal that can be connected to the phone line. A church might leave an evangelistic game on the computer in the evenings so that people with home computers could call in just as they telephone a dial-a-prayer message.

"I heard about a church in Texas," Pastor Skeptic says, "that used a computer to telephone every number in the phone book with a recorded gospel message. Rather than being good evangelism, that turned many away from the church."

There are, however, some very constructive ways to use telephones in combination with computers in outreach and evangelism. Another church in Texas uses a computer to assist with a more productive telephone evangelism program. The church office computer keeps accurate records of newcomers and visitors. Members who have volunteered to make phone calls receive each week, via computer telephone call, the names, telephone numbers, and other information about people they are to call and invite to participate in the activities of the church.

Radio and television evangelism is often more effective when information gained about the audience from mail or other responses is computerized. Much of this computer use, however, has focused on fund raising to sustain the broadcasts. Other potential uses of computers for evangelism in relation to the broadcast media have hardly been explored. There is some evidence to suggest that, with computers, two-way radio and TV broadcasting may make possible a more effective use of media for evangelism. The Rev. Gabe Campbell, for example, found that he attracted a different kind of audience when he listened to people, hearing them voice their concerns and problems on the air, instead of just preaching at them.

The effectiveness of media evangelism can be founded upon sophisticated computer analysis of audience responses and participation. What really interests nonchurch viewers? What really moves them?

Not only can the computer make it possible for the church to follow up and keep in touch with people who respond to radio or TV broadcasts, but computers can also help to make the content of radio and TV evangelism more relevant and effective. Those who plan media evangelism can proceed with more confidence in two-way, interactive audience involvement when they have ready access to the resources of computer data bases.

The quality of evangelistic presentations can be improved with computer graphics and music. An ability to make the high quality evangelistic presentations described in the following section will make it possible for churches in the United States to follow the lead of churches in Europe and Canada where teletext and videotex presentations of the gospel are prepared by denominations and local congregations.

Art and Evangelism

"No," says Pastor Skeptic, "I don't know anything about the capacity of my Commodore computer for creating music, graphics, or art. I'll leave that to others."

Certainly all pastors and church members will not learn all there is to know about every possible church application of computers. But some will want to explore ways that the computer can be used in the production of art and music.

Some churches and many church members own videotape recorders and video cameras that can be used with computers to create astonishing new kinds of presentations of the gospel and of the work of the local church.

It is possible that some of the people who are not reached by evangelism efforts today would respond better to artistic presentations. In the Middle Ages the church encouraged artists to communicate the gospel in nonverbal ways. Indeed, words alone can be shallow, half-empty proclamation. Art can often express feelings, emotions, caring, and deeper dimensions of faith better than words do. And this may be especially true in the future as the computer and related electronic technology open up entirely new kinds of art.

The gospel might be presented through locally produced television programs that use computer graphics and titling or teletext and videotex presentations.

The Jehovah's Witnesses have demonstrated the effectiveness of bringing a phonograph record into a home during an evangelistic call. With computer assistance churches could prepare videotape presentations that could be taken by church members into the homes of prospects as part of an evangelism visit.

"Isn't it much easier just to rent a film or tape?" asks Pastor Skeptic. Commercially produced artistic presentations will continue to be easier to use than those produced by a local church. But the locally produced presentations may better accomplish the desired results. One of the most effective forms of evangelism, of course, is for people to provide a personal witness by telling their own stories or the story of their own church. With computer assistance, very professional yet personal presentations can be prepared by a local church.

Global Outreach and Mission

"How can a congregation use a computer for global outreach and world mission?" Pastor Skeptic asks. "I suppose the answers are by fund raising for missions and by including missions education in computer-assisted instruction. But more than that? We try in all we do to keep members reminded of the church's global mission."

Some parishes are already using computers through The Source or other electronic mail connections to keep in touch with foreign missions officials. "Soon," one pastor says, "I will be able to transfer a catalog of special missionary projects from the computer in the denominational headquarters into the church's computer. This year our Vacation Bible School children are raising money for a tractor in Africa. Computers can keep track of which project is accepted by which church, and the people who are raising money in Nebraska can use a computer network and satellite communications to communicate with the church people who receive the tractor in Africa.''

Some congregations have established special relationships with congregations in other countries, including young people's visits, pastoral visits, and gifts. Others are keeping in touch with missionaries through ham radio. American churches have for a long time supported overseas radio stations for use in evangelism and have experimented with TV programs in mission lands. Many of the major electronic church broadcasts in the United States are sent to other lands by satellite. As the use of computer technology in American churches is developed, opportunities will occur to help churches in mission lands adapt the technology to their needs.

Computer networks have the potential of drawing Christians into closer and more immediate contact and fellowship across international borders. Such new means of electronic communications can make it possible for Christians in different countries to be more supportive of each other's efforts at witness and service and supportive of justice and human rights. Information and messages from a computer in Texas can be sent directly to a computer in the Philippines. Indeed, this long-distance communication already occurs in the process of translating the Bible into Filipino dialects. It is likely that parish churches in Europe and America will become more closely involved with missions as this potential is discovered and used by more and more laypersons.

Some American congregations and Christian individuals are already contributing computers to a church office in Africa and to a Baptist university in the Philippines. Such electronic equipment may be much more important for churches in mission lands than for congregations in America for the extension of the gospel. There is a real danger that information-age technology will be used by totalitarian governments and colonialists to oppress third-world people. Just as churches have supported the rights of people around the world to have adequate food, clothing, and shelter, so churches can also work to insure fair and adequate distribution of information. Often this will be an extension of mission work being done today. The only chance some third-world Christians have to share in information-age technology may be through church-established data banks and computer networks.

One of the important mission tasks of the near future will be assisting churches around the world to adapt to changes that result from the introduction of computers. The task will be to help "give a voice to the voiceless" so that Christians in other countries can use the new technology to speak for themselves. American Christians may be able to create alternatives for people everywhere to bypass those who may seek to monopolize information-age technology for the first world's profit alone.

Local churches will need to learn about the issues related to information and communication as they affect mission work. Support of the New World Information Order (the effort of third-world people to get a fair hearing from the world's news services) may be one of the most important activities a local church mission committee will be involved in, in the years ahead.

Richard Hirsch, secretary of the Communications Department of the U.S. Catholic Conference, says that the importance of the decision to establish church satellite communications systems is of comparable importance to the church's decision to build parochial school systems. Computer-satellite networks can bring increased power and influence into the work of overseas church colleges and their mission institutions. It is possible that such a sharing of electronic technology with churches overseas may catch the imagination of American and European Christians as much as the building of mission hospitals, schools, and agricultural stations did in the last century.

Dr. Judy Hinds points out that church use of computers as a tool for world-wide communications and global consciousness will require careful study of existing communication patterns, a respect for limitations, a willingness to reallocate resources, a commitment to training, and a determination to identify new sources of expertise and financial support.

For More Information

See Thomas L. McPhail, *Electronic Colonialism: The Future of International Broadcasting and Communication* (Beverly Hills, Calif.: Sage Publications, 1981). Rodney Booth, *The Winds of God,* (World Council of Churches, 1982), asks how the churches will respond to the challenge of computer technology, citing Juan Rada, "The Microelectronics Revolution: Implications for the Third World," *Development Dialogue* (1982) II. The "First Asian Workshop on Church Planning to Use Computers," *Resources for Communications* (Dec. 29, 1982), recommended (a) the development of cadres of hardware and software specialists to advise churches, (b) "computer camps" for church leaders, and (c) exchange of information and technology between churches in different countries. The World Future Society, 4916 St. Elmo Avenue, Bethesda, MD 20814-5089, has audiotapes: "Transferring Technology to the Third World" and "Communications and the Third World."

Checklist

Would your church use a computer to:

—find prospective members by computer use of house-by-house survey information and records?

—help follow-up on parish calling campaigns and other evangelism efforts?

—correlate U.S. Census information about area of parish responsibility?

—match names of prospective members with those who would regularly cultivate their interest?

—form special interest groups around personal needs?

—use more effectively public media: radio, TV, Teletext, and newspapers?

—make a more sophisticated analysis of responses to church outreach, such as broadcasts?

—use computer graphics to prepare more attractive outreach materials and mailings?

—use computer networking to keep in touch with Christians all over the world?

Computer Graphics

The symbols a computer manipulates can be shapes and colors that appear on a TV screen, dots that are printed out on a dot-matrix printer, or instructions to a device called a plotter that draws lines on paper. The ability of a particular computer system to do graphics depends on both the hardware and the software. Many of the less expensive computers sold for home use can be used to create sophisticated designs on a TV screen, and some printers will print out whatever is viewed on the screen. Graphic designs, once created on the computer, can also be stored on a disk for later use. Realistic pictures, titling, cartoonlike animation and graphs can be produced on paper from a screen with the aid of a computer.

Teletext

Teletext is the continuous transmission of information over telephone lines, a cable TV channel, or an FM or TV broadcast channel. A computer decoder makes it possible for words and pictures, called a "page of information," to be viewed on a TV screen. With a computer decoder costing less than $100, British viewers can choose information from 250 pages of text on topics such as stock market, weather, and news. This technology, now under experimental use in the United States, may have a great potential for church outreach.

Using Computers
in Parish Education

Use computers in religious education?" Pastor Skeptic shook his head. "Programmed instruction and computer games have no place in the church. I've seen experiments in using machines to teach kids, and maybe machines are good for drills in math, but religion must be taught by warm, loving persons."

The role that computers will play in education in the future is not clear, but certainly religious education can never be turned over completely to a machine. As Dennis Benson, whose imaginative educational materials have been widely used by congregations of many denominations, has written, "The computer applications in education will only be fresh and vital if we take the gift of human interaction as a serious legacy of God. The computer must always be seen as a handmaiden to the teacher who can be even more available to aid the student."[1]

It is ironic that church educators, who affirm the uniqueness of individuals in God's creation, have done so little to discover the peculiar gifts and needs of each individual and use them as the foundation for improving religious education. Or perhaps it is not, since local church leaders have not hitherto had instruments and procedures that were adequate for keeping such compehensive records.

The use of computers in the Sunday church school classroom will grow slowly because computers represent a large investment in equipment that will be used only one or two hours a week. In the immediate future the use of home computers as part of the Sunday church school program presents problems because all homes will not have computers and because different brands of home computers often use different software.

Yet computers will have an important impact on religious education because computers force the asking of important questions about both the goals and methods of religious education.

The education leaders of a congregation generally have goals, sometimes rather vague or unexamined, which are used as guidelines for selecting materials and establishing programs and plans. So the place to begin in deciding whether or not to use computers in religious education should be with these goals. In many churches the first benefit of considering computer assistance with education will be the careful examination of educational goals.

Many of the applications described in previous chapters can be used to assist educational ministry. One area is in recruitment.

Education Recruitment

One church has used its computer to organize old minutes of the Christian education committee and, in doing so, has found that important ideas have often been lost. One recurring problem was how to involve young people who had dropped out of youth work or church programs. From computerized membership lists and education records a list was prepared of persons between the ages of twelve and thirty. The computer tallied their actual participation and other available information about them with some surprising results.

For example, many of these inactive younger people had volunteered at least once to participate or help on an occasional basis, and the offer had been lost or forgotten. It was the church that had been disinterested, rather than the young person whose college, Sunday job, or military responsibilities made it difficult to assume regular duties. Many of these people were pleased to be asked to serve as a substitute teacher or to attend a special program. (With a computer, a system of periodic reminders could be set up with a calendar to invite such people to be involved on a pattern of their own choosing.) Next, the religious education committee was able to interest some of them in a personal reading program for furthering their religious growth wherever they were.

Curriculum

As a church begins to think about computer use, it may look for a software curriculum, designed and ready-made to do everything the printed curriculum presumably has done. But today, and perhaps for a long time in the future, a comprehensive computerized curriculum does not exist. Individuals, parishes, denominations, and commercial firms have created and will continue to produce educational software, but this software is not likely to fit together in any coordinated plan, except as such a plan is developed by a congregation. Of course, this is not an entirely new situation. Many random activities are planned in church school and youth activities that may or may not really help achieve the goals set by the parish education committee and its curriculum. But at the present time computer assistance needs to be seen as a way to enrich the church's educational ministry.

There may never be curricula that use computers to replace the printed text and activity books used in Sunday church schools because the greatest benefit of using computers and information-age technology in education is that these new tools make it possible to move educational initiative back to the individual. Mass-produced religious education curricula made possible great advances in religious education, but they assumed that all persons are much the same and can be taught in the same way. The best use of computers in education builds on the fact that each person is an individual with unique educational needs. Computers can assist with the task of adapting and tailoring materials to meet the specific needs of individuals and groups in a congregation. The development of Sunday church school curricula was necessary because teachers needed to be provided with very specific material with which to work. But computers make it possible to use many kinds of educational resources. Each student can be provided with educational materials that are specifically suited to his or her needs. Materials used with a group can be designed for the needs of the group.

Before a Sunday church school program can take advantage of vast educational resources to develop individualized programs, information about individuals needs to be collected.

Comprehensive Records

Parish leaders have assumed that church school teachers can adapt and tailor curriculum to fit the needs of a class and of each individual child. In some cases, of course, Sunday church school teachers have done so brilliantly. Specially tailored programs have been created for blind, deaf, mentally retarded, abused persons and others with obvious needs. For the most part, however, teachers have not had adequate information about all their children's special needs, talents, and problems; nor have church teachers had the time and means to obtain a profile of each person.

By a profile of a person, we mean a gathering together of all that is known about that person's religious life and development. Dennis Benson, in an article entitled "FAKE CAT: The Computer as Medium and Message," asks, "What about exploring the dreams and undeveloped areas of a person's life? The computer can enable us to lift up an amazingly complex analysis of individuals. . . ."[2]

These comprehensive records can be used to develop profiles of Sunday church school classes and can provide a teacher with statistics that will make it possible to prepare relevant and appropriate programs. Parish education leaders need help in developing Christian commitment and deeper faith in particular youngsters. Computers might be able to help.

Most of us feel that a physician would not be acting responsibly if he or she proposed a program to meet a youngster's health needs without an examination of the child and his or her medical records. Churches could do a better job in education if they kept more comprehensive records on each person, although they already have some information that they do not use. Granger Westberg, a Lutheran pastor who has served on a medical school faculty, has experimented successfully with "holistic health care" programs in churches. These programs treat the whole person and the entire family with a team that includes physician, pastor, and others. This experience suggests that religious educators might learn from Lawrence Weed, M.D., who suggests that holistic records be kept which include much more information about family, school experience, and so on.

In the future a profile of a young person—his or her commitments, faith, attitudes, evaluations of experiences—may be built up automatically while he or she plays computer games or participates in computer assisted instruction. Currently there are computer games that collect information about the game player—how a youngster learns and how his or her psychology may be affecting learning—for educators to use.[3] In the future, similar games may be developed that will collect information that can be analyzed and used for more effective religious education.

Comprehensive records could also be used to help individuals. A youngster might come to the church computer lab for an annual spiritual checkup. This birthday event would be a time for an annual updating of the church's computer profile, which records all church involvements and Christian education achievements. On each birthday the youngster would be encouraged to use the computer to review goals set the previous year and to set new spiritual-growth goals for the coming year. The computer program, by asking a series of challenging questions and by reviewing various possible activities for the next year, could help both youngsters and families be more aware of what is or is not happening in their spiritual development.

Computer-Assisted Instruction

A number of computer-assisted instruction (C.A.I.) software packages are coming onto the market in the field of religion. A bulletin of one of the church computer user's organizations recently listed over a hundred of them. Some are very fundamentalist, some very liberal, some educationally naive and amateur. Some are also quite well done. Many C.A.I. programs are most useful to individuals who want to study on their own.

C.A.I. can be used to do some of the tasks that teachers would be doing anyway. Thus teachers would be able to give more time to individuals. A computer game that drills the names of the books of the Bible might be used rather than a game that involves the teacher. Or C.A.I. can be used by the teacher as an aid just as flannelgraph boards or overhead projectors are used. For example, a computer-created animation could be used to illustrate the story of Jonah as the teacher tells the story. But the use of computers in education has far more potential than merely putting workbooks on the screen and asking pupils to use a keyboard instead of a pencil.

One exciting future possibility of the computer in education involves its use with the video disk to create textbooks and programs that are interactive. Parker Rossman visited the World Computer Center in Paris in May and June, 1983, to investigate progress in the creation of the textbook that can talk to a pupil and answer questions with motion pictures, graphic art, or music. He learned from Arthur C. Clarke, who invented the space satellite, that we are much closer to a portable electronic tutor than most educators realize. The computer-video disk player that is being developed in Paris can answer questions from a vast electronic encyclopedia. One video disk can contain 55,000 encylopedia pages. An electronic tutor is being developed to teach agriculture to illiterate farmers in West Africa, and this technology can be used by the church. A pastor in Iowa is experimenting to develop such an interactive program for studying about Luther.

A major advantage of C.A.I. is that it can be interactive. This means that it responds to the directions and sometimes the needs of the learner. For example, one electronic tutor shows a youngster how to repair a bicycle. The film can be played slowly, frame by frame, or replayed over and over so that the youngster can carefully watch each step in the process. To ask a question, a youngster has only to touch the screen at a point in the film that is not clear to bring up more detailed instructions. Some manufacturers are now preparing such programs so that people can repair their own furnaces or appliances. C.A.I. programs are already being used by surgeons who can stop a film of an operation to ask the computer for more explanation.

Some people believe that religious education will not use such sophisticated computer programs in this century because if the programs are really well done, their production can be as expensive as a Hollywood film. Churches have never made effective use of movies or TV for the same reason. Yet many congregations and their youth groups have been involved in filmmaking that has been very educational for the persons making the film. It is in this spirit that some local church people are now creating their own experimental software for educational use. This software may not be as sophisticated as commercially produced software, but much is learned in the process of producing it.

"Since it's hard to get adults together for any sort of training class," says Pastor Hopeful, "I look forward to the day when anyone in the parish can come at his or her convenience to use a C.A.I. program for individualized instruction on how to usher, make a hospital call, teach a class, or chair a committee."

C.A.I. Sex Education

An interesting illustration of how computers might be used to enlarge home-church collaboration in religious education was an experimental C.A.I. sex education program conducted at a church in Dallas.[4] The curriculum was prepared by a theologian at Southern Methodist University and was used in a regular junior high class. The young people did their homework at computer terminals in Dallas that were connected to a large Control Data Corporation computer in Minneapolis.

"Homework?" One can hear Pastor Skeptic laughing already. "It would be easier to pull their eyeteeth than to get junior high church school pupils to do homework."

In fact, the young people in the sex education class did so much homework—often with their parents—that no such group had ever come to the church so well prepared. The computer did not "teach" but simply provided resources for teachers, parents, and pupils. The computer was programmed to be an interactive textbook that could answer questions so that the pupil avoided embarrassment and received confidential answers. But the most important aspect of the course was the way the computers got parents, who often avoid the subject, actively involved in the learning, the teaching, and discussions with their children. The post-course evaluation found that the C.A.I. program had helped the junior high young people to make more responsible decisions about sexual activities, helped them to be more comfortable with their own sexuality, and helped them understand that sex is a normal part of their lives.

A next step, made possible by video disk technology, will be sex education programs tailored to a particular youngster. The computer can be programmed to give answers in keeping with the different values and commitments of each family. Suppose, for example, a youngster asks what percentage of young people are engaging in sexual intercourse before age sixteen. The computer—in a way that parent or teacher might find difficult to do, without seeming to nag—could respond accurately to such a question while persistently reminding the youngster of the perspectives of his or her faith and family on the question.

Papert's LOGO

LOGO may turn education upside down. The LOGO computer language, designed for children's education, is described in Seymour Papert's book, *Mindstorms: Children, Computers, and Powerful Ideas*.

Papert spent many years at M.I.T. working on computer technology while simultaneously studying child development with Piaget. He laments the fact that most people use computers for games, entertainment, or business. They overlook the fact that computers can affect how people think and learn. Papert believes that computers can help cut across the lines that have separated physical sciences from the knowledge of the self. "Only rarely," Papert says, "does some exceptional event lead people to reorganize their intellectual self-image in such a way as to open up new perspectives. . . ."[5] These new perspectives are possible because, according to Papert, computers help learners free themselves from methods that have spiritually and intellectually crippled pupils in the past.

LOGO is a computer language for children to use to learn about mathematics and the physical world in the same natural way that they learned to speak their mother tongue. Children who use Papert's computer programs are not taught the laws of nature. They are helped to discover laws for themselves. They learn truth they cannot as yet put into words.

Christians have always known that our faith summons us to a lifetime of personal spiritual adventure; yet religious education has so often surrendered to mass-produced, assembly-line approaches to knowledge and learning. Papert's studies suggest that computers need not be used only for drill and rote learning. Computers may bring an end to trivialization and trite answers in religious education that have often alienated people and closed minds. We might think of properly programmed computers of the future as partners in spiritual journeying.

Papert has made another observation about the potential of computers in education. Computers can be thought of as machines always ready to be taught. The LOGO language is specifically designed so that children can quickly become proficient in teaching the computer to draw shapes and designs on a TV screen. As children become more proficient with the language, they can teach the computer sets of rules in order to govern the way it will respond. Papert's experiments demonstrate that when children learn to take control of the computer and direct their own learning, they then "establish intimate contact with some of the deepest ideas . . . from the art of intellectual model building."[6]

Computers might be used in the same way in religious education. By teaching a computer the model of one's understanding of reality, contradictions and areas of unclear understanding would be discovered. Today Papert's proposals have been implemented in a language to help children learn about the physical world. In the future someone may build on his ideas to develop a computer environment in which children can make discoveries about spiritual reality.

Footnotes

[1] Dennis Benson, "FAKE CAT: The Computer as Medium and Message," *Military Chaplains Review* (Spring 1983), p. 64.

[2] *Ibid.*, p. 65.

[3] *Ibid.*, pp. 61-66.

[4] Parker Rossman, "The Future of Sex Education," *The Futurist* (December 1983).

⁵ Seymour Papert, *Mindstorms: Children, Computers, and Powerful Ideas* (New York: Basic Books, 1980), p. 43.

⁶ *Ibid.*, p.5.

For More Information

See articles on education in *Byte* (August 1980); World Future Society tapes: "What Really Will Happen As Communication Devices Revolutionize Education," and "The Child as Electronic Learner"; Parker Rossman, "Technological Communications and the Churches," *Listening* (December 1983).

Checklist

Would you use a computer to:

—prepare computer-assisted programs for Sunday church school, youth work, and membership instruction?

—build up profiles of comprehensive information on each pupil for better counseling and planning of religious growth?

—study attendance records, do better follow-up on dropouts?

—develop a handbook of procedures from cumulative minutes of religious education committee meetings?

—inventory teaching materials and simplify procedures for ordering curriculum?

—aid in teaching?

—develop better follow-up of youth away from home, in the army or college?

—test and score tests?

—conduct an annual program of spiritual checkup?

—assist teachers in preparation?

LOGO

When children use a computer programmed in LOGO, they can command a "turtle" (a device for drawing) to move right or left, forward or backward, in order to make squares, triangles, or increasingly complicated shapes and images. As well as creating a continually challenging and expanding learning environment, this learning language excites children with the discovery that—instead of being intimidated by the computer—they can take control of and manage this sophisticated technology. They can use it to solve problems, to learn by doing, and to discover their own ways of learning and thinking.

Using Computers to Enrich Religious Home Life

Many church families now have computers and related electronic technology at home, and many more soon will. One forecaster predicts that a decade from now most homes will have a system of interrelated devices—several TV sets, including one with a large wall screen; videotape recorder; radio; stereo sound system; audiotape recorder—that will provide a new range of educational, religious, and cultural-entertainment possibilities. At the heart of this home entertainment system will be one or more computers. This comprehensive system will make it possible for people to create as well as to be entertained. Children will not be limited to watching whatever cartoons are broadcast at the time when they want to be entertained. They might create their own cartoons, using a computer to make animations and sound effects. They will be able to request that specific cartoons be sent to them over a cable system, and they might have a library of cartoons in the home from which to choose. The same system that is used for entertainment might be used for education and enrichment. It is as yet too early to know the impact of computers on home life, but it seems fairly safe to predict that many more people will be doing their work at home. The home will become the place where people work, learn, and play.

Another result of having so much technology available may be a reduction in a family's dependence upon schools, churches, and other institutions. One denominational official recently said that the denomination might become little more than a toll free number for people to call to ask about resources available for home use.

We do not believe that the ''electronic cottages'' of the future will completely take over the functions of the church. People need to gather to express and share their faith. Nor will the life of Christians become so home centered that individuals from many households will not join together as the body of Christ.

We recognize that there are many dangers to families as radical changes are brought about by computers and related technologies entering the home. Christian families and the church must carefully assess each new possibility. But we believe that there are ways that computers and related technology can be used to enrich home religious life. We agree with Myron Berger, who wrote in the September 27, 1982, *New York Times,* that computers are beginning to make the home into a much more responsive environment, far different from any human habitat in the past. Computer-designed environments can in time be created so as to reflect and promote the chosen goals and values of those who live there.

Will Computers Be like TV?

Professor Louis Forsdale of Columbia University Teacher's College, speaking at a September 1983 consultation on information-age technology in church and school, reminded his audience how wrong Margaret Mead had been when she predicted that the coming of TV would end the fragmentation and dissolution of the family. She was sure that families would gather around the TV set and discuss programs they watched together. In fact, TV seems to have caused a decline in family conversation as individuals go off to watch different TV sets. And as computer equipment for entertainment becomes more sophisticated, there is a danger that religious and educational activities at home will continue to decline in quality unless churches and schools initiate new cooperative programs and plans with the home.

One of Forsdale's colleagues has suggested that computers will reenforce extroverts to become more extroverted and introverts to become more introverted. We believe that computers will have similar effects on families. Computer technology will fragment some families and draw others together.

The impact of computers on home life needs to be watched very carefully. On September 15, 1983, the *New York Times* reported the beginning of a major, two-year, foundation-funded research project to study how computers affect children's learning and motor skills, relationships between generations, and the quality of family life. The researchers noted that this study will be similar to studies of the impact of TV. It is expected that there will be quite different results, however, because TV elicits a passive response while computers make it possible for a person to exercise control.

Home Education

Professor Mary Alice White, director of the electronic learning laboratory at Teacher's College, Columbia University, told consultants at a May 4, 1983, meeting on the role of churches and education in the information age that American parents will soon be spending about six billion dollars on computer hardware and software. This means, she said, that most of them will be buying educational packages that are not part of a coordinated curriculum. The result is likely to be the production of what Professor White calls "confetti heads," children who are able to withdraw information from a computer data bank but who have "no way of putting it together in a chronological sequence or a meaningful context against any kind of background."[1] Since market research projections indicate that parents will be spending ten times what the schools will spend on computer materials, parents will be taking much of their children's education out of the hands of the school. "Education has moved out of the school into the television set . . ." Professor White said.[2] Adults and young people are increasingly doing much of their fundamental learning at home.

This places a new opportunity and a frightening responsibility in the hands of the church to help parents in this tremendous educational undertaking at home. Professor White said to church people, "You better become electronic educators and you had better become leaders at it. Because if you don't, you're going to be by-passed."[3]

Professor White's address was followed by an address given by Timothy Gunn, who is responsible for educational courses on a public broadcasting station. He raised the issue of quality, saying that it will be very difficult for a coherent curriculum design to emerge from a decentralized system of educational technology development. "Who," he asked, "brings the needs of learners and teachers to the Silicon Valley software specialists?"[4] Who sets the standards and does the evaluation of materials that a family may buy?

Ultimately each family will be responsible for the decisions that are made about the purchase and use of educational materials in the home. But in the years ahead, a local church can offer support and resources to families as they face the additional responsibility. Churches can offer workshops to help families prepare and experiment with their own computer religious education programs. In addition to offering ideas for family computer activities for special days like Christmas or Easter, such a workshop may help a family begin to prepare a computerized family history. Software is now available to encourage families to preserve their own religious traditions and ancestor stories.

Many children will not be able to afford the cost of using computer networks and data bases for research. The cost of using computer data bases, on-line encyclopedias, and files of major newspapers and magazines for homework could be a hundred dollars a month. But alternative church networks and data bases could provide families low-cost access to religious information. A church library may, therefore, want to begin making plans now to develop its local data base in cooperation with member families.

Computer Games

Every computer game has a religious dimension. Each game supports certain values. Each family will want to evaluate carefully the games that are used in the home. Are they consistent with the values that are important to the family?

Card and board games have long been a part of family life. Computer games can fill a similar role. But as computer games develop in depth and educational value, they can offer more to a family than these traditional games. With a computer game there can be family togetherness just as there is with a board or card game, but the level of skill expected from each player can be controlled by the computer. This means that it is possible for a five-year-old child to play on equal terms with an adult.

Another potential advantage of computer games is that they can be played over a number of days and even when family members are away from home. For example, a chess game played on a board must be set up in a specific place and is usually played in one sitting. But a chess game played on a computer can be played over a period of several days without danger of having the pieces spilled. If one of the players must be away from the home, the game can still be part of the life of the family as moves are telephoned into the home computer.

Computer games are already available to help children and adults learn about religious subjects. Surveys show that the big market for computer programs for religious instruction is likely to be the family, not the church. Church libraries might lend computer games and programs for members to use on home computers. One reason to use computers for Sunday church school and youth programs will be to introduce young people to religious computer programs that they can borrow and use at home.

Home Organization

Calendar programs are available for most home computers. A family can use these programs to keep track of commitments and plans. The computer can also help the family evaluate the way time is spent. A family could, for example, keep a computer record of rather simple activities as a basis for evaluating its commitment to its values. Much could be learned, for example, from a cumulative record of the TV programs watched or of the way the home computer is used.

Software to help the family with money management is also available. With this software all expenditures can be monitored. Since the computer can quickly generate reports, the family can analyze whether the way money is used is consistent with the family's values.

One function of the family's computer will be that of reminding. Suppose, for example, a family has decided to play some devotional tapes every morning during breakfast. Such resolutions are often forgotten because other activities intrude. The computer, however, will not forget. It will keep track of the tapes and start the right one at the right time each morning.

The home-computer-controlled tape deck can make possible a new approach to devotional materials for children. Babies and toddlers can be nurtured by a specially designed program of religious songs, play suggestions, and taped stories. Electronic stimulation can never replace the important role of loving adults that surround a child, but computer control of electronic devices can improve the quality of electronic stimulation a child receives. A half hour of listening each night can provide 1800 hours of listening time between birth and age ten.

Computers will also allow a greater degree of control over the use of other electronic stimulation in the lives of children. Computer control of television cassette recorders can ensure that programs are not missed because they are broadcast at an inconvenient time.

Family Profiles

In the previous chapter on religious education we suggested that many congregations will use a computer to collect and coordinate information about individuals as a foundation for developing a tailored program for religious growth, designed to meet each person's unique needs and possibilities. In the next chapter we consider ways that computers can help with counseling. In the future, churches may be able to use computers to combine information about individuals to help them solve many of the problems that now lead to divorce and family disruption. Family profiles could be prepared and used as the basis for selecting and preparing materials for family enrichment at home. Family profiles would not be used to tell a family what to do. The profiles would be a tool to give a family insight into ways to enrich its life.

In the future, software may be available to help families develop a model of the way they function. This model could be used to help a family understand family dynamics. The model could also be compared to models of other Christian families. These models would not be "ideal families," but they would be examples to help a family better understand the possible effects of working to change the family's life-style.

Christian Family Networks

When a group of American families lives overseas at a place where there is no American school, the parents often plan together to share resources to educate their children. Family clusters are also developing in the United States with families working together through supportive networks. As suggested in the 1984 book *Family Survival*,[5] clusters may become an important new style of Christian family life. Some are suggesting that there may be no other way for Christian families to survive in the coming electronic jungle.

Churches can use electronic bulletin boards (described in chapter 2) to help families discover other families with similar needs or interests. The information collected by the church can be used to link families that might not otherwise come into contact with each other. Computer dating services have existed since the 1970s to bring together people with similar needs and interests. Groups of families who have members who are terminally ill, handicapped, senile, or mentally ill can be clustered by using information collected by the church.

The church computer can also be used to provide resources to families. Families in the church would use the church's computer not only to obtain information about services but also to report on services and give evaluations so that others can determine whether a particular service is appropriate. In this way the church can make it possible for more senior citizens to stay in their own homes and reduce institutionalization and hospitalization of other people.

Footnotes

[1]Mary White, "Education in the Information Age: The Role of the Churches," *Report of a Consultation* (New York: National Council of Churches, 1983), pp. 10, 11.

[2]*Ibid.*, p. 10.

[3]*Ibid.*, p. 11.

[4]Timothy Gunn, "Education in the Information Age: The Role of the Churches," *Report of a Consultation* (New York: National Council of Churches, 1983), p. 13.

[5]Parker Rossman, *Family Survival* (New York: Pilgrim Press, 1984).

For More Information

American Family, newsletter on family policy and programs related to the National Center for Family Studies at Catholic University of America, Cardinal Station, Washington, DC 20064, has a regular column on "Families and Telematics." The September 1983 issue reports on the Center for Family Studies, Box 835, Cambridge, MA 02139, which uses the computer to diagram genealogical relationships and to produce extensive chronologies of family events. The World Future Society offers an audiotape, "People, Families and Communities in the Communications and Information Era," (90 minutes) and others on the family in the computer age.

Checklist

Would you use a computer to:

—form computer networks of Christian families?

—help families make better religious and educational use of their home computers?

—coordinate curriculum and spiritual-life programs at church and in the home?

—help church families keep records of spiritual growth and development?

—implement devotional and educational materials for children at home?

—provide computer-literacy instruction for families who have no home or school computers available?

—provide coordinated services and help for families with special problems?

—send religious materials and information to homes via computer networks or computer bulletin board?

8

Computers in Pastoral Care and Counseling

$\mathbb{P}$astor Skeptic was almost angry. "Now don't tell me that some congregations are preparing to use computers as counselors!" We hope not, although what Arthur C. Clarke said about teachers may well be true of pastors also: any pastor who *can* be replaced by a computer *should* be replaced by one.

Pastoral counseling must involve a warm human relationship. But almost any counseling, no matter who does it, can be improved with more accurate information. And computers can help counselors store and organize information. Computers might also make possible new forms of self-help counseling.

Pastoral Counseling in the Computer Age

Many pastors already are using a computer to organize their calendars and work for more efficient parish administration so that they have more time to be personal with individuals. A few use their computers to maintain schedules of devotions and to remind them of persons who have requested prayers. Some are using computers to keep records of pastoral needs, to make sure they follow up on promises and intentions. A computer cannot make a pastor more sensitive, thoughtful, responsible, or prayerful in pastoral care, but computer reminders can be very helpful to a pastor.

Dr. Stanley Lesse, author of a book on the future of health care, says that physicians must become more pastoral. An educator, describing computer use in the classroom, says teachers must become more pastoral—more personal in their demonstrated caring. Pastors, too, can have more time to be personal as they turn some routine work over to computers, but they can also become more professional. A professional pastor does not practice a skill as a mere technician but as a human being who is conscious of dealing with other human beings in the complexity of human situations. In our time, the complexity is becoming so overwhelming that many pastors can manage all that they ought to do in pastoral care and counseling only with the help of computers.

Collecting Information

Computers have been used effectively by counselors in the routine gathering of information. This often saves the counselor time. A more important advantage is that with the computer asking routine questions, the counselor can be a friend rather than an interrogator. Dr. Kenneth Colby of the University of California used a computer with people who found it easier to respond about some embarrassing or difficult problem to a computer than to a human counselor. A computer, Colby pointed out, has no facial expression, no superior social status, and makes no moral judgments. But a computer can never show real caring as a human counselor can. There will always be times when a counselor will want to demonstrate a caring attitude by participating in collecting information.

The church computer can also be used to keep track of counseling that has been done.

A medical educator, writing in the *Futurist*, said that computer systems will be developed to take histories which are infinitely more detailed. We believe religious leaders will be able to "piggyback" on the medical trend of holistic preventive medicine, which requires partnership between family, school, church, and others in dealing with problems such as drug and alcohol abuse.

The computer may not only make it possible but also in time make it mandatory for a pastor or religious counselor to use records much as a physician does. A doctor knows that a patient could be seriously harmed or even killed if medication were given without accurate records of a person's previous medical history. One young pastor learned this lesson a hard way, when a person he was counseling committed suicide as a result of advice he gave without adequate information about the person's background.

Analyzing and Diagnosing

Kenneth Colby worked with scientist Joseph Weizenbaum to develop a computer program that would "provide a communicative experience intended to be therapeutic. . . . designed to communicate an intent to help, as a psychotherapist does, and to respond, as he does, by questioning, clarifying, focusing, rephrasing, and occasionally interpreting.''[1]

Colby's computers could respond, as a counselor does, with stock answers such as "Can you elaborate?" or "Tell me about your feelings." But Colby reported that nearly everyone who tested the·program found machine counseling to be frustrating and annoying because the responses were so limited.

Another problem with Colby's computer counselor was that the computer program did not have a conceptual model of mental health against which the appropriateness of responses might be judged.

Colby's experimentation later demonstrated that specialists could develop computer models describing, for example, the characteristics of a paranoid so that a patient's responses might be compared to the model. The computer cannot actually make mental health diagnoses. It can only report that the responses made by a certain individual are similar to responses that the person who prepared the model would expect from a person suffering from paranoia.

Computer programs to aid with pastoral counseling are already available. There are computer programs for professionals to use in cases of drug or alcohol abuse, in stress management, in marriage counseling, and in areas of mental health.

Richard and Joan Hunt, at Southern Methodist University, have developed a computer program to help pastors in counseling. The computer-assisted exploration exercises can be used in considering several areas of marriage. The computer programs invite each partner to respond to several types of situations and then the partners compare their responses and discuss them. The counselor can then discuss results with the couple and use the experience with the computer materials as part of premarital or marriage counseling.

Pencil and paper are currently used to complete MIRROR, a couple relationship inventory also prepared by the Hunts as an aid to couples in examining both content and process dimensions of their relationship. The answers are scored and profiled by computer. The couple then has the profile and an interpretive guide to use in discussing issues that are identified. The Hunts plan to make this inventory available as part of computer-assisted counseling. With the computer, the couple can compare their backgrounds, note differences and similarities, develop proposed spending plans, and check their knowledge of many areas of marriage.

The Hunts are also using computers to explore communication skills of couples; they converse with each other via computerized scripts and then receive results of how well they express affection and how they deal with power in their relationships. In the same way that computers are used to score personality tests and other inventories, the Hunts' computer-printed profile provides scores on ninety-six scales and correlates other information in ways that would be impossible without a computer. The Hunts are also developing computer-assisted instruction materials for couples to use as a supplement to the United Methodist marriage book, *Growing Love in Christian Marriage.*[2]

An Iowa pastor has been working on the development of a procedure for an "annual spiritual examination," an idea suggested by annual physical or dental examinations. Such a diagnostic counseling session, which perhaps a congregation could propose as an annual birthday event, could uncover problems before they become serious. However, taking clues from the holistic health movement, the focus would be upon growth and healthy development.

There are computer depression inventories, temperament analyses, and various versions of Minnesota Multiple Personality Inventories. But who is qualified to diagnose spiritual problems or to evaluate spiritual growth? As yet there is no answer to that question. Individuals must set their own spiritual goals and seek the help of spiritual guides in undertaking their own evaluation.

It is rare for anyone to have serious discussions with children about their personal religious goals, spiritual progress, and plans to enrich and develop their spiritual lives. Records of counseling with adults are also rare. Without records religious counselors are hampered in their efforts to help a member or family at a time of special need. A computer can keep a record of the time when each child or family is counseled on spiritual growth as well as when there is sickness, behavior problems, or crises. A minister in Hawaii uses his computer to keep track of each pastoral visit or extended conversation. The computer can periodically produce a list of everyone in the constituency who has not received regular spiritual guidance.

Self-Help Programs

As yet there are no adequate software packages for computer-assisted instruction in counseling for lay people or clergy. When they are developed, it will be essential for churches to evaluate these materials and provide guidance in their use. It is possible that C.A.I. programs to train church members in counseling skills will greatly improve the quality of the counseling that church members give to others.

By 1983 "do-it-yourself" programs for stress management, assertiveness training, dream interpretation, and self-analysis were available. People who now use books for such purposes will soon be buying more sophisticated computer packages. *American Family*³ foresees, for good or bad, many families using home computers for self-diagnosis of their problems. Some are questioning the wisdom of making computerized self-help resources available to everyone. Professor Weizenbaum is fearful of software that intervenes in the psyche of the patient, especially because there is no way of controlling who buys the program and how it is used.⁴

Referrals and Resources

A computer can help the church with counseling by making sure that the best up-to-date information is available for referrals. The church should be much more than a booking office that refers people to various agencies for counseling and help, but often the church provides the most help to people with serious problems by referring them to the wide range of agencies available in American society. For an alcohol- or drug-abuse problem, for example, there are tax-supported counselors and centers that can provide highly skilled assistance. And a church would waste time and money if it set out to duplicate job-search facilities provided by a tax-supported employment office. The parish instead can direct people to those offices and services, using its computer directory and other computer directories in the community to find the best help available. The parish's own computer directory would include the names of church members who could provide special counseling or help in areas in which they have specific expertise.

There are times when the counseling ministry of the church identifies similar problems being experienced by a number of people.

One church decided to try to help unemployed persons. Establishing a computer job bank, the pastor reports, has involved more members in the process of job seeking for others. Members are eager to help with the project because they know that the computer will keep track of all information that is provided. Computer organization insures that every suggestion is passed on to the persons most able to make good use of it. The computer also assists with matching job possibilities to unemployed persons, sorting out information to communicate it to unemployed members, and coordinating the sending of information to persons who may help with recommendations, transportation, encouragement, or job training. The computer keeps a record of every effort an unemployed person makes. This record provides a sound foundation for adequate job counseling as well as for counseling to keep up the morale of the unemployed.

Another kind of computer-enabled teamwork, as illustrated by the job search for the unemployed, mobilizes all members of the congregation to do better what they are doing anyway: sharing information with each other. Canadian churches are using TELIDON, a computerized bulletin-board system broadcast over cable television to publicize telephone numbers of people and agencies that can provide counseling and other assistance. Much information can be provided electronically, just as the telephone company now gives recorded information in response to many questions. In many communities, people can telephone legal or medical agencies where a computer will provide information for them—taped messages with standard replies to many frequently asked questions. Churches can now begin to offer similar services.

Pastors may soon use a portable computer terminal when making visitations in order to record case histories and to provide people they counsel with information from computer data banks. It is no longer necessary to return to the church office for names and numbers of recommended services. A small computer printer could be used to print out a list of agency telephone numbers, for example, to leave with a family. The technology allowing pastors to provide such a service is already available.

Privacy and Confidentiality

There is often concern that confidential information can fall into the wrong hands. Computer records can be safeguarded just as written records can be safeguarded. Some church and counseling software packages include special features to limit access or protect confidentiality. However, as Philip Estridge, the president of IBM's personal computer division, has pointed out, "I guarantee that whatever scheme you come up with will take less time to break than to think of it."[5] A congregation's considerations about long-range computer use should, therefore, include some provisional guidelines about its use. Guidelines may suggest that some kinds of records be kept only by the pastor and should be available only to him or her. As with other records, the pastor will want to sort them carefully when moving to a new position and decide what information should be shared with the new pastor. The only way to insure the confidentiality of counseling records is not to store them in the church's computer system where unauthorized people might discover how to read them. How then, you ask, can pastoral counseling benefit from a comprehensive record or profile of each person who is counseled? We suggest that each comprehensive record be the property of the individual or family and should be kept on a computer disk at home. It can thus be coordinated with school, medical, and other records as well. This disk would be made available to a pastor or other counselor as part of the contract for receiving pastoral counseling. While even this system might be abused, it places the responsibility for what information will be shared on each individual.

Footnotes

[1] See George Alexander, "Terminal Therapy," *Psychology Today* (September 1978), p. 53.

[2] Richard and Joan Hunt, *Growing Love in Christian Marriage* (Nashville: Abingdon Press, 1981). For more information, write to the Hunts at P.O. Box 8265, Dallas, TX 75205.

[3] "Experts Say Role of Mental Health Professionals to Change Dramatically with Use of Home Computers," *American Family* (September 1983). This article says that before the end of the decade most American families will have home computers with a wide choice of programs, including a great many self-help programs in physical and mental health. A variety of programs are in various stages of development and testing, for example, in drug and alcohol abuse and stress management and marriage preparation and analysis. Already many family counselors are using such computer programs in self-administered assessment tests.

[4] For a fuller explanation of all the reservations which Joseph Weizenbaum has, see his *Computer Power and Human Reason: From Judgment to Calculation* (San Francisco: W.H. Freeman, 1976).

[5] Lawrence J. Curran and Richard S. Shuford, "IBM's Estridge," *BYTE* (November 1983), p. 96.

For More Information

Prevention magazine (September 1983) reports on computer and videogames to help young people cope with serious disease and to counsel on preventive health. See also "Measuring Attitudes with a PST," *Byte* magazine (July 1982); Phyllis Wollman, "Small Computers in Medicine," *Popular Computing* (October 2, 1982). The Educational Testing Service has a computer program for vocational change counseling.

Checklist

Would you use the computer to:

—keep better counseling statistics, such as who has been counseled by whom and when?

—ask preliminary questions in counseling for the gathering of essential background information?

—help shy persons who can confide better in machines?

—help in computer-assisted instruction of lay and peer counselors?

—help counselors keep more professional records as a step of excellence in counseling?

—help set up programs to meet specific needs found in counseling, such as job finding for members in times of acute unemployment?

—organize a calendar of counseling appointments, including a regular schedule to invite people to meet for counseling before problems become serious?

—coordinate information about counseling materials and resources?

Using Computers
in Preparing Worship

Pastor Skeptic shakes his head. "Now surely our worship committee will have no use for one of those computers except perhaps to keep statistics on attendance and to keep track of minutes. But I might want to prepare sermons using a word processor when the secretary is not using the computer to prepare the weekly worship bulletin."

Certainly computers cannot participate in worship. The seminary student who programmed a personal computer to print prayers on a television screen while he attended class did not understand Christian worship. Those who plan public worship, however, need to give attention to creating the proper environment for worship. A computer can help with worship administration, with worship instruction, and in creating an environment for worship. Just as electronic organs make it possible for congregations to have beautiful music to assist them as they worship, computers can be used by people to help plan and control the environment of worship.

Some people resist the notion that worship should be carefully prepared at all. They feel it should be entirely spontaneous. Therefore they resist using a computer in planning worship. We agree that there are times when the Spirit directs worship that has not been planned. But there are other times when God is glorified because careful attention has been given to planning worship.

Members' Participation and Response

One congregation found that attendance at worship significantly improved after a computer was used in a program to invite members to take turns in the planning or conducting of worship. The computer was used to prepare schedules of people to serve as door greeters, soloists, acolytes, and so on. Churches have often set up schedules for worship participation. The advantage of using a computer is that it can keep track of each person's participation to ensure that everyone is involved. The computer can also help in the selection of people who participate together, pairing a new member with a member of long standing or a young person with a senior citizen. Once the schedule is in the computer, the church office can automatically send out the assignments and reminders.

The church with computerized schedules of participation discovered an increased congregational interest in the preparation of worship. The pastor began holding meetings each Tuesday of representative groups of members in order to discuss the next week's sermon. The pastor found these Tuesday meetings helped in training lay leaders, and he was helped as they studied the Scriptures together and discussed the needs of people that might be addressed in the sermon. The computer helped in the sorting process, keeping track of people's interest and participation. It became possible for the pastor to invite people with special interests related to a particular sermon topic. For example, if the pastor planned to preach on peace, the computer could help to bring together members who represented different viewpoints on military preparedness.

Worship Environment

Computers can control lights, furnaces, and air conditioning. At a conference on church use of computers a number of pastors asked about using computers to control heating and lighting. They were primarily interested in saving energy costs. Specially designed computers can be used by the church for this purpose.

Some pastors are beginning to realize the exciting potential of the computer in creating environments for worship that can change each week according to the liturgical season. It would be possible to have the church cold and dark when people arrive on Easter and then to have the room explode with light and joyous music at the shout "Christ is risen!" A computer can be used for timing and controlling all of the elements in a drama.

In the 1960s many people were involved in experimenting with the correlated use of strobe lights, films and slides, rock music, and other special effects to create dramatic worship experiences. The creation of unusual services involved lighting experts, composers, projectionists, actors, and dancers. That experimentation provided the groundwork for careful planning of all elements of public worship. Computers now make possible the fuller use of people's creativity in art and worship. The experimentation in the 1960s may well have been a prelude to problems and possibilities ahead for the church as culture and art become increasingly electronic.

Computers and Music

Some cultic churches have been experimenting with the use·of sound and images for shock effect to stimulate and accelerate the experience of salvation. Manfred Clynes of the New South Wales Conservatory of Music in Australia has been using a computerized device for a decade to produce compositions that mix sounds and feelings together, just as a painter mixes colors.

Many young people are devoting themselves to popular music. They compose and create their own music and electronic effects using computers to coordinate sounds, lights, and graphics to appeal to all of the senses as do opera, ballet, and high church liturgy. Can congregations encourage such creative use of computers for music and art?

Creative Computing magazine reported that the Radio Shack company is attempting to create a new breed of musicians by offering inexpensive software that anyone can use to compose music on a TRS-80 computer. With this software one can record a composition on tape and play it directly through a stereo system. It does not matter whether the young composer can read music. The 1982 manual with the software package made it possible for almost anyone to be programming music within a few minutes. The manual included an example of sheet music converted into Micro Music coding.

The process of composing is amazingly simple. To shift from one octave to another, for example, the composer simply presses the SHIFT button on the computer. There are similarly simple operations for selecting rhythm and speed. One can listen to the notes as they are typed on the computer keyboard, and it is easy to make changes or corrections. This software is, of course, hardly an introduction to the more sophisticated software now being developed for the creation of new kinds of music.

Not only has the computer created a revolution in how composers think about music, but computerized equipment also makes it possible for almost anyone to do remarkable musical things: computer-assisted music analysis and sound analysis, computerized musical data structures. Youngsters can begin composing almost before they have any instruction in music.

The magazine *Music and Sound Output*,[1] for example, is addressed to people who are interested in using electronics to create popular music. This may sound unrelated to church music, but advertisements in the magazine offer computerized equipment that composers of religious music can use. For example, a computer system that can transpose music, can orchestrate instruments, and edit arrangements is described. MPC's Music Percussion Computer links a Timex computer to a TV set to show a graphic display of rhythms. Another computer device, Music Teacher in a Box, teaches theory with a compact, calculator-style package that will show which notes to play with a given note in order to make chords in any key. The Casio CT-405 can create the sounds of a hundred instruments, including a pipe organ.

Helen Bonny has suggested in *Music and Your Mind* that music can reach into deeper levels of consciousness and higher dimensions of religious experience.[2] We know that music can have healing qualities, that there is some special relationship between music, spirituality, creativity, and God. But church people have been slow to notice how computers can be used to bring exciting new dimensions of music into the worship of even small, impoverished congregations. Congregations in impoverished rural areas of the Philippines sometimes make better use of electronic technology in their worship than do affluent American congregations.

Yamaha organs now exist with computer features for recording and creating special music. They can use prerecorded materials much as did player pianos. Average congregations have long encouraged, trained, and nurtured young musicians to become organists, choir directors, and even composers. They can now encourage their young musicians to learn to use computers to enrich Christian worship with significant new forms of art and music.

Organization of Worship Resources

Most churches cannot take full advantage of the music resources they have. Pastors and members do not know what music resources the congregation has—recordings for the children's choir, choirbooks and sheet music, organ and instrumental music—or where these resources are. Rarely are these musical resources indexed according to the liturgical year or themes that a pastor might use in sermons. Many of the software systems designed for churches include programs to help organize the congregation's music library.

A computer-indexed music library could include music and other kinds of worship materials—poems, prayers, Scripture passages from various translations, litanies, and alternative liturgical forms. All materials can be organized with a comprehensive theme index.

All music can be coordinated with other plans in ways never before anticipated or appreciated. A worship committee and pastor can thus use the computer to avoid unintended duplication or repetition in the use of music or other worship materials while at the same time drawing from a much larger and richer variety of resources.

Architecture

Architects, through the use of computers, can create better the construction design that a congregation wants. One congregation used a computer to involve nearly everyone in the congregation in the planning of a new church building. People were invited to watch a computer monitor as alternative styles and space uses were presented through computer graphics. Reactions were then tallied on the computer. Parish leaders were not surprised that young people planned a youth activities room with great enthusiasm, but without the computer's correlation of responses they would have overlooked the deep interest that many of the young people showed in the design of sanctuary windows, chancel lighting, and acoustics.

We have come a long way from the days when nearly everyone in the community helped with the construction of great medieval cathedrals or with nailing shingles on the roof of a small rural church. Even though there is evidence that people make better use of and have greater appreciation for buildings they have had a hand in planning, it is difficult to involve many people in planning a building. Because computers can sort and organize many suggestions, it is again possible to involve the whole community in designing church buildings.

Worship Evaluation

A computer can be used in various ways to evaluate services or sermons. People can be invited to pause at a computer terminal in the narthex after the service to record suggestions and comments. One congregation found that some people who were too busy after service on Sunday to answer a computer questionnaire would return later to type in their answers to the evaluation questions. This, of course, required one computer to be set aside almost exclusively for this use. A computer can be used to organize any questionnaire results. A worship committee might want to learn which sermons and services appeal only to one age group. It might try to pinpoint which aspects of the service are inadequately prepared or performed. Better use of the results of a questionnaire is possible when a bar graph or other graphic presentation is prepared using a computer. No one knows enough about worship needs and interests of most congregations because pastors and leaders have not had the kinds of tools of evaluation that computers can provide.

Information about worship participation can be collected over the years. Analysis of such data can provide the pastor or worship committee with guidance for worship preparation.

A pastor in California uses a computer to correlate information about participation in worship with data about the season, weather, and make-up of the congregation. Computer projections of the size and makeup of the congregation for the next Sunday are used when the service is planned.

Telecommunications and Worship

Materials for devotion were provided for computer users in the spring of 1982 via The Source, the *Reader's Digest*–owned information utility. Such computer service might be compared to dial-a-prayer on the telephone. It represents a religious presence in the national electronic information utility. A local church could distribute meditations using bulletin board software and the office computer when the church office is closed.

Telecommunications technology makes it possible for pastors in different towns to exchange texts of next week's sermons and to get constructive criticism. It would also be possible for pastors to share in developing a collection of illustrations on the lectionary text.

Weddings, Baptisms, Funerals

One pastor begins premarital instruction by showing on his computer monitor the various options and choices the couple has in planning the wedding service. He finds that if the computer program asks the questions that ought to be asked about the meaning of the vows the couple are making, he can assume a pastoral rather than instructional role. He says this makes it easier for him to present items that his church requires or to deal with difficult problems that may arise in the instruction.

He prints out a copy of the service for discussion. If the couple wants music, poems, or readings in the service, these can be displayed on the computer screen or printed out from material that has previously been stored on the computer. Suggestions made by the couple of poems or readings can be typed into the computer. During the conference the pastor types decisions made into the computer. A completed copy of the service can be printed and given to the couple as they leave. If they wish to memorize some of the vows, they then have the printed copy. The personalized printed copy of their marriage service also becomes a memento.

The same procedure can be followed in consulting with a family about a funeral, a service of home dedication, or a baptism, making it possible to present options and to give the family a printed copy for their records of what is agreed upon.

Footnotes

[1] *Music and Sound Output*, 220 Westbury Avenue, Carle Place, New York, NY 11514.

[2] Helen L. Bonny and Louis M. Savary, *Music and Your Mind: Listening with a New Consciousness* (New York: Harper & Row, Publishers, Inc., 1973).

For More Information

One's imagination about electronic environments might be stimulated by "Planetary Theatres," *The Futurist* (December 1982) and by the World Future Society's audiotape "Arts and the Image Reality" (90 minutes).

See Gabe Campbell, "Consensus of the Faithful," *New Catholic World* (May-June 1978) on computer feedback to sermons; "Connecticut Minister Using Computer to Sample Congregation's Opinion," *New York Times* (January 17, 1978); Parker Rossman, "Parish Feedback," *Christian Century* (October 10, 1979).

Checklist

Would you use a computer to:

—create computer music or art for worship or train young people to do so?

—organize the church music library and correlate it with other worship resources?

—involve more members in worship preparation, leadership, and evaluation?

—design special worship environments with computer coordinated films, sounds, and so on?

—keep track of prayer requests?

—conduct computer-assisted instruction in advance of weddings and other special occasions?

—place prayers or devotional materials on computer networks?

—involve members in sermon preparation?

—draw upon worship resources via computer networks or data banks?

—consult via computer networks with other congregations on sermons or worship?

Using Computers in Service and Action

©hurch action and community service can be empowered and improved by use of information-age technology. A congregation can use its computer to find people who will serve, to help train and equip them, to support their efforts, and to help reduce divisions and tensions that many congregations experience when they seek to act upon controversial issues.

Dr. Judy Hinds and Brother Austin David Carroll are typical of the people who are experimenting with ways to use computers in the church's ministry of service and action.

Judy Hinds, of the computer task force of the Nuclear Weapons Freeze Campaign, says that the use of computers for military purposes has raised serious questions about "whether this technology will play a positive role in moving toward a human world order. . . . Fortunately," she says, "there are signs that computers have a significant role to play in the search for alternatives. Whether the technology is used appropriately depends very much, though, upon our clear understanding of what needs to be done and how computers might help."[1] Most of us have become accustomed to thinking of computers as devices only for numerical computation or information processing and retrieval. Hinds says, however, that when the computer is combined with interactive communications the results can be surprisingly compatible with the values required for a human world order.

Brother Austin David Carroll established the Pope John Paul II Center of Prayer and Study for Peace in 1982 under the sponsorship of the Roman Catholic Archdiocese of New York. After he studied computer technology and instructional strategies at New York University, it occurred to him that computers could be used in planning for peace as well as for war. Brother David hopes to establish a global information resource that will use computer organization of peace information and satellite communications and make this information available to people working for peace.

Brother David recognized that more is required to prevent wars than for churches to gather and share information. He has proposed, therefore, to use computers to train skilled peacemakers and to undertake a long-range process of research to discover and help develop effective alternatives to war. In other words, he is suggesting that the church use computers to play peace games as the Pentagon uses them to play war games.

Brother David says that data and theories modeling an incident could be fed into a computer so that the computer could predict a logical succession of events if certain things happened. He shows how one can build simulation models. If the enemy takes action A, then the other side will take action B and the result will be action C because the data base tells us that 95 percent of the time actions A and B result in C. Brother David hopes to use this method on problems like those in Northern Ireland. The church could thus use computers to train and equip third-party negotiators to seek to prevent aggression. At present, he says, even our church decisions on political and social questions are too often made on the basis of gut reaction rather than on a careful analysis of fact.

Computerized networks of information and simulations such as those being developed by Hinds and Carroll may be available in the future to help with conflict resolution within a nation or in a community. Their initial efforts to use computers to build world peace include involving people in the process, collecting information about contributions individuals have to make, establishing computer networks, and using teleconferencing. All of these uses of computers and related technology can potentially be used in local churches.

Involving More People

Richard Spady, a Methodist businessman in Seattle, Washington, became concerned in the 1960s over the divisions in parishes in the midst of the great pressures of that protest decade.[3] Some people were dropping out of congregations because they saw church people being apathetic, not caring that many of the world's children were hungry, not acting to reduce torture, injustice, and discrimination. Other church members were angry because they did not agree with what church leaders were doing and saying, in the names of their churches, on political and social issues.

Spady began to use computers to involve more church people in the decision-making process. He organized people into groups to learn about issues and to discuss them. Computers were used to tally and communicate the decisions of many such groups. Spady sees, in this process the possibility of better church leadership because the leaders can obtain input about decisions from their constituency through such computer use.

Spady feels that computers may help to mobilize a higher percentage of church members in decision making as well as in human service. A congregation's purchase of a computer, therefore, can be a step towards two-way participation in denominational affairs. The old style of directives from the top down to a congregation in matters of action and service can be replaced by a system that considers input from the membership.

Spady found that electronic technology can help to move people from a passive to a more participative style so that the average member can understand more about what is happening and can become more involved.

Congregations have often used questionnaires to ascertain what action or service projects members wanted the church to undertake and what the members themselves were willing to do to help. Response was often limited, however, because people knew from experience that the parish was not prepared to make use of such information. Computers can now change that, helping church leaders to organize, correlate, and use such data well. Computers can help congregations use data instead of merely gathering it.

People who disagree are often silent when social issues or action projects are discussed at large church meetings, unless they get angry enough to walk out. A voice can be given to these silent people by the use of the computer consensor, invented by W.W. Simmons.[4] The consensor provides each participant with a button to push at any time to indicate agreement, disagreement, or the need for more information.

This computer consensor has been used by parishes to increase democratic participation, especially by those who are silent because of shyness. It can speed up decision making because as soon as persons push buttons indicating agreement, it reports that consensus is reached. It has been used also in biblical and theological discussion to get involvement of people who otherwise do not speak. Spady has found that if people feel they are heard and understood, then they can support the church in controversial actions even when they may disagree.

Another way a computer can help to involve more people is by using it to identify people who would likely respond to a particular situation. For example, the United Methodist Board of Church and Society was committed to the principles and passage of the Equal Rights Amendment to the Constitution. Methodist women's groups had for several years been provided with study materials on ERA and related issues. The efforts of the national board, however, were hampered by the need to identify people in Methodist congregations who were interested in working in support of the ERA. This could have been solved by keeping a computer record of all people who wrote or telephoned for information about ERA. Such a list could then have been computerized by location so that if the legislature in Illinois were preparing to vote on the ERA amendment, the computer could quickly prepare a list of every Methodist in Illinois who would want to be informed. The computer could sort the list by county or seek out the names of a few key people in each congregation in the district of a legislator who was trying to make up his or her mind on the issue.

Interest Banks

In a local church an interest bank could be established to make sure that people are contacted about issues that interest them. Chapter 6 discusses the establishment of computerized talent banks of church members. The talent bank can be expanded to include an interest bank to help people with common interests get in touch with each other. Perhaps, for example, a pastor finds a member who would be interested in making jail visits for the church but does not wish to do so alone. Computer sorting can help to find others with the same interest.

One Connecticut congregation surveyed its members to ask how they might be willing to help others in an emergency. The survey found that most members were already more involved in community service than the pastor realized. Some members wondered where they could get more help for projects on which they were already working. What members needed was coordination of their efforts. A businessman in the parish used his computer to match people with similar needs and interests, thus helping many more members become actively involved in the kind of service they wanted to undertake.

Church action groups often waste time and money sending mass mailings to people who only discard them. A computer can be used to target people in the parish who would be most likely to want and use materials. The general church mailing list may become a thing of the past. It will be replaced by collections of names and addresses, each coded for interests so that every mailing from the church office will be of interest to those who receive it. It has been proposed to the nuclear freeze campaign that there be no national mailing list but, rather, a mailing list of area and local leaders. These leaders should be given access to microcomputers so that they could prepare their own local mailing lists. A computer can sort such lists to match legislative districts.

Both conservative and liberal political groups and community-based organizations have demonstrated the effectiveness of computerized mailing lists for fund raising. Certainly the churches will not want to fall behind as various special interest groups promote less worthy interests

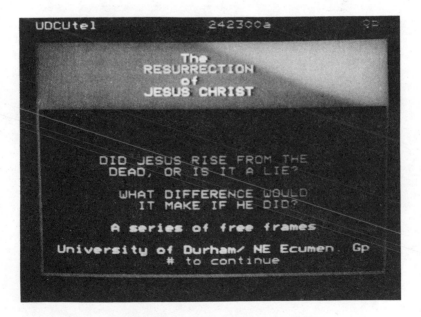

Sample of Screen of Videotext Material

in the society. Computers and related technology will change the ways in which churches act to promote their concerns.

Computer Networks

Computer networks such as those being experimented with by Brother David at the Center of Prayer and Study for Peace will soon be providing information to people in local churches. The computer in the local church can connect through a modem and the telephone line to a computer, in another city, that stores the latest statistics and information about what other people are doing.

Soon it will be possible for a church action committee to use a computer to get information from libraries, from commercial data banks, or from denominational headquarters and to have the latest facts on pertinent issues. It will be possible to obtain this information, if necessary, while a meeting is in progress.

A denominational office may, therefore, want a computer system that can be used to provide information to many congregations. Church computer consultant Robert Cramer[5] says that during the next few years it is going to be essential for churches to make careful plans for information storage and retrieval systems that can be easily used by the average church member. Cramer feels that, for the present, church networking should use commercial systems, such as The Source. He says that there are dealers ready to sell the equipment needed for churches to set up their own computer-to-computer networks but that now is the time for study and preparation, not purchase. Any denominational network formed now would be plagued by snags, clutter, and delays and would need replacing in a few years. Its operation might require specialized knowledge that the church would not have at this time. On the other hand, computer networking through a commercial service such as The Source could benefit the church immediately.

Brother David's Center of Prayer and Study for Peace is moving ahead with plans to establish a network for the church. This network would allow church members to make use of over 10,000 entries in the West German Institute for Theology and Peace.

Teleconferencing and Computer Bulletin Boards

Sometimes there are emergencies, unusual opportunities, or surprises by the opposition, says Judy Hinds, that call for increasingly complex and rapid responses. Through computer conferencing, people scattered around the country can hold consultations and meetings with a greater likelihood of immediate and effective feedback and coordination. People traveling or working on the same action project in different parts of the country can use portable computer terminals to keep in touch with each other despite hectic schedules and time-zone differences.

The church has always had both formal and informal networks of people. Computers and telecommunications technology offer a new medium for these networks. Judy Hinds suggests the use of the Electronic Information Exchange System (EIES) to help people gain a greater sense of community. Through this computer-based communications system, over 700 people in North America and Europe send and receive messages, engage in computer conferencing or meetings, jointly draft articles and reports, read computer-based journals, and create computer aids tailored to their own work needs.

Dr. Murray Turoff, designer of EIES, has called it a "blooming buzzing garden"[6] wherein over fifty groups have been working on cooperative projects, one of them a religious network. Turoff says that eventually there will be dozens of computer networks like this, linking people all over the country and abroad around common interests, involving many thousands of people in joint research and action. EIES, initially available for $66 a month membership, operates on minicomputer technology and is relatively inexpensive compared to the telephone and most other kinds of communication.

Judy Hinds observes that there is freedom from limitations of sex, age, race, discipline, disability, and schedule or organizational differences with teleconferencing. Computer conferencing permits easy creation of new kinds of groups for special purposes. It can increase the variety of ideas brought to bear on an issue, including perspectives from many parts of the country and world, while at the same time helping people feel that they are part of a community of common interest that need not be geographically based. In a friendly and often unexpectedly intimate environment, participants see that they become members of a community. Computer conferencing is really a new social invention.

Scattered participants in an action project can also be kept up-to-date on developments by a computer bulletin board. Regularly updated announcements can be made about special meetings, programs, legislative alerts, and so on. The information can be transferred to anyone who has a connected computer, appearing on screen as community announcements appear on cable TV. In fact, the same announcements could automatically be transferred to a cable system for that purpose.

Any person having a computer printer could make a copy of the announcements on the screen. This hard copy could be used as a poster, in a newsletter, or sent as a release to a local newspaper.

A congregation may want to set up its own electronic bulletin board to communicate with members who have computers. Such communications can be bi-directional to assist parish leaders in becoming more sensitive to community needs.

Social Action in the Computer Age

The style of social action in the 1960s and 1970s tended to be confrontational or radical protest. The action style of the computer era is more likely to be one that seeks to relate people with common interests through networks. Most social action will be done at the local level, sharing national and international information and strategy. This is the style of Richard Spady, who uses computers to convene small discussion groups to help people inform and express themselves on crucial state or national issues.

The church also needs to remember that its prophetic witness in the world is to be guided by the demands of the gospel rather than by popular opinion. Computers can only help to organize and distribute information, thus facilitating communication.

Computers and telecommunications may end the scarcity of church news in the public media, says Shirley Koritnik of Kansas City *Ecumedia*. Using computer networks, the church can collect and distribute news around the country and the world. This news will bypass the antireligion bias of the large news services. Each local church can distribute news to local media.

The introduction of computers into society may provide the greatest impetus for the church to become involved in social action. Will computer technology only be available to the rich? Some congregations are using their computers to help poor youngsters to enter the computer age and train themselves for computer jobs.

The global issues may be more serious. Robert Jacobson, at the 1980 Pacific Communications Conference in Hawaii, warned that "power elites" want to reserve computer communication facilities for themselves exclusively and do not intend to make access to them universally available. If this happens, democracy will falter and a new permanent underclass will develop with most people ending up worse off than they are now, Jacobson predicted. The alternative to tyranny, indeed, may be the network of computers in churches.

Footnotes

[1]Correspondence with Judy Hinds. Judy Hinds's proposal for a computer system task force is unpublished. See Judy Hinds, "Communications and World Order," *Breakthrough* (Summer 1983) and "Susanna, The National Seminar's Electronic Friend," *Response* (January 1984).

[2]Austin David Carroll, "Can Computers be used for Peace?" *Media Development* (UK), vol. 30, no. 2.

[3]Richard Spady, 628 West Lake Sammamish Parkway N.E., Bellevue, WA 98009.

[4]W.W. Simmons, Applied Futures, 22 Greenwich Place, Greenwich, CT 06830.

[5]Robert Cramer, Resources for Communication, 341 Mark West Station Road, Windsor, CA 95492.

[6]Conversation with Murray Turoff, New Jersey Institute of Technology, 323 High Street, Newark, NJ 07102.

For More Information

The address of the Pope John Paul II Center of Prayer and Study for Peace is 7-8 State Street (South Ferry), New York, NY 10004. The World Future Society offers audiotapes on "Communications for Peace," "Networking and Communication for Peace," and "Networking and MetaNetworking: An Overview" (each 90 minutes). There are many articles on this topic in the *Futurist* magazine and in reports of its conferences, held at 4916 St. Elmo Avenue, Bethesda MD 20814-5089. *Reach Out and Touch* is an introductory guide to electronic conferencing by churches and religious organizations, written by Rev. Paul Kearns of the Annenberg School of Communications, University of Southern California, and Sister Elizabeth Thoman, director of the Center for Communications Ministry in Los Angeles.

Checklist

Would your congregation use a computer to:
—recruit, train, and support service volunteers?
—help shy persons express their concerns?
—create an interest bank to facilitate service and action?
—help people to find others with common action interests?
—provide an electronic bulletin board?
—send mailings to raise funds for action causes?

—organize and mobilize volunteers for an action campaign?

—set up computer conferences for working with people across great distances?

—do computer modeling to try out an action strategy before implementing it to see what actual consequences might be?

Being Faithful in the Computer Age

Should churches buy computers? If so, how can a church decide what is needed? Is the purchase of a computer just another business decision to be made?

A national consultation late in 1983 found that advice is difficult to give because hardware and software prices and features continually change. Thus it is almost impossible to put good advice into print. One cannot trust published reviews of software and certainly not the ads of the retailers or manufacturers. So the most appropriate advice we can give is for purchasers to check with others who have been using specific programs or equipment for evaluations of performance. One may find such people through groups like the Church Computer Users Network,[1] which has a quarterly newsletter containing lists of sources of church computer software and articles written by people who are using computers in churches.

Dr. Ronald Lien of the Control Data Corporation suggested to a church conference that religious bodies can react to the computer revolution in one of four ways: 1) they can resist the technology and the ramifications of its use; 2) they can ignore the technology for a time; 3) they can accomodate the technology, sitting passively while secular forces use computers to affect and influence the churches; or 4) they can pursue the use of the new technology and gain the experience and expertise necessary to make significant use of it in order to achieve the goals of the church and of Jesus Christ in human society. Can church people have faith, he asked, to see computers as something given by God to be cared for and used, to see that God is present in all technology as in all nature?

Church Consultants Needed

Churches need consultants who can give informed advice about computer systems for parish use. Just as a church uses an architect to ensure that plans for a new building are cost-effective and consistent with the needs of the congregation, so a church uses the services of a computer consultant. A parish making large expenditures for a system to do sophisticated tasks will probably need a continuing relationship with a consultant.

Experts who will advise churches on hardware and software purchases do exist. But who certifies them? Do they really know enough about church programs? Are they giving sound advice? Denominational and ecumenical agencies should set up comprehensive workshops and training programs. Denominations should be finding people to train and certify as qualified consultants.

Meanwhile, as in pioneering areas of church life in the past, many congregations will need to begin by finding and training people from their own membership, just as they do when they need someone to operate a movie projector.

Strategy—Hot Line

For the most part, denominations do not have a strategy or long-range plans for entering the information age. They have no sense of mission, no call to claim either the technology or the emerging new computer age for Jesus Christ. National church leaders often seem to be interested in computers only for the purposes of administration, fund raising, and institutional survival and do not show the sense of adventure, the willingness to take risks that often characterized missionary movements in the past. We asked several prominent theologians for answers to some of the questions in this book, and all of them said that they knew nothing about computers and their implications.

Leadership in the computer age for the church must come from people like yourself working in local churches. Retired people and youth have special contributions to make.

Dennis Benson, who is experimenting with the development of theologically sound yet exciting computer programs for youngsters, feels that computers will make a highly significant contribution to the life of the church by helping to find and to make use of talents of laypeople.

"The faith family has probably the greatest collection of talent on earth," he says. Yet in most settings these talents have been very little used. He adds, "The thirteen- and fourteen-year-old young people who are helping me develop religious video games have much to give."[2]

Denominations can best meet the needs of parishes for computer advice by facilitating the exchange of information between people in different local churches. As different parishes experiment with computers, each will gain bits of expertise that they can share with other congregations. Since much of the best computer software for use in religious education may for some years be produced by laypeople using their own parishes as laboratories, a way to distribute these materials is needed. Information-age technology is changing the traditional procedure in which church agencies provide help from the top down. Denominations could establish offices with toll free telephone numbers or computer bulletin boards. These offices would be places where pastors and laity could call with information about successes and difficulties they are encountering. They could serve as clearing houses to help people make contact with others in the church who are interested in the same issue. Many of the answers to questions would come from the bottom, that is, from parish experience.

Computer-Age Problems

Being faithful in service to Christ will require churches to help individuals and society cope with stress created by the computer age, including the stress that results from changing work patterns. This will require a comprehensive Christian overview of what is happening in the world. Many Christians have used Alvin Toffler's *The Third Wave* for help in understanding the revolutionary nature of changes in their lives. Toffler sees history moving through an agricultural era, then a traumatic industrial age, and now an even more upsetting information age.

In the industrial age experts waited until they had enough evidence to back up their position before making a pronouncement. This was true for theologians and church leaders as well. Now, however, the information age is moving with such speed that all Christians are called to take some risks and to share with each other whatever theological insights or guidance they have at the moment. Pastors and laypeople, therefore, need no longer hesitate to speak to the church and the theologians. We are all in the same boat, nearly swamped in the stormy sea of change described by Toffler.

Christians, however, must see beyond Toffler's third wave to a fourth. The agricultural wave involved a quest for security in organized production. And once some economic security was achieved by the industrial age, humanity began to develop science, education, and information for all. As that effort climaxes with the arrival of the information age, Christians can proclaim the need for society to prepare to move on to the next wave—spiritual revolution—so that people can make more humane and loving use of production and technology. If we have the vision, the church can begin to lead the way into the fourth-wave society, based on love and focusing on the development of the potential of the human personality. The signs of the beginning of the next wave can already be seen. Yet where is the readiness of the church to receive it, to lead it, and to shape it?

Those who focus instead on consolidating and building upon the third wave are devoting themselves, for example, to efforts to use computer technology to give society more mechanical brain power, when what is needed is more compassion and love power. More brain power by itself is likely to be applied to using computers to create more terrible weapons of war, torture, and oppression. Can church people begin to find ways to use powerful new electronic tools as Paul used writing and as Luther used books, not merely to empower the brain, but to empower ethics, love, vision, and faith?

A fundamental issue in the church use of computers is not the tools, even frighteningly powerful electronic tools, but the layperson's understanding of the role of the church in society and human history. Computers will reshape human society no matter how church people respond and act. The question is this: How aware will laypeople and pastors be of how computers are changing society and of how God calls them to respond and act in the midst of this highly seductive information-age revolution?

We have said that the initiative in preparation of software for religious educaton has passed into the hands of laypeople and pastors who experiment locally. So also the initiative in the development of theology to interpret the information age may be passing into the hands of laypeople in the parish.

Test by Gospel

There are no easy tests to apply to a particular computer use to determine whether it is consistent with the gospel. There are no easy answers to computer-age values questions, as people become aware that computers will change their work, churches, schools, and other institutions. How can Christians be more alert to the gospel implications of computer uses in secular areas of society? For example, it is very dangerous to give a computer the power to determine when and if to begin a nuclear war.

The gospel will lead church people to ask questions about the ecclesiastical uses of computers. How is efficiency versus fellowship to be weighed in deciding whether to computerize a task that has traditionally been done by a group of people gathering at the church? If a handicapped volunteer has enjoyed doing a repetitive chore for the parish, should the task be given to a computer that can do it faster and with greater accuracy? If computers reduce the need for office help, should the church seek to find other jobs for its displaced employees? Or should such laypersons be employed for other, more personal, ministries?

The church can raise a prophetic voice in society by seeking answers. Such questions must be answered in much of society. Christians are less likely to be heard on these issues, however, unless church leaders are conscientious in their own computer planning and evaluation, taking careful account of the gospel in decisions about whether to purchase and how to use a computer system. In many situations it may be wise for a parish not to move too quickly into computer use. This does not excuse the pastor and leaders of that parish, however, from responsibility to equip themselves to minister to and with people who are experiencing changes in their lives because of the introduction of computers in society.

Even some computer people in the parish may wish that the church would remain an island unaffected by the information age. But in most cases the church will be more faithful to its purpose if it is equipped to talk about and to understand computer-age issues.

At a West Coast conference on church use of computers, Richard Johnson of the Exxon Foundation, a Methodist layman, cautioned against getting bogged down in transient issues. He compared the church's present situation to its position in the years prior to the nearly universal availability of TV sets. The important question, he said, is, What will we do with the technology? There is a call for vision in using computers as communication tools to help the church to reach people and to explore and transcend time and space.

Footnotes

[1] Church Computer Users Network, Box 1392, Dallas, TX 75221.
[2] Dennis Benson, "FAKE CAT: The Computer as Medium and Mes-

sage," *Military Chaplains Review* (Spring 1983), p. 65.

For More Information

See Michael L. Dertouzos and Joel Moses, eds., *The Computer Age: A Twenty-Year View* (Cambridge, Mass.: M.I.T. Press, 1979); G. Friedrichs and A. Schaff, *Microelectronics and Society* (Elmsford, N.Y.: Pergamon Press, Inc., 1982).

The Research and Statistics Unit of the United Presbyterian Church found that 75 percent of the congregations owning a computer or very interested in getting one expected costs of at least two to six thousand dollars. Of the computers that had been purchased by churches, 25 percent had been purchased with special gifts, 45 percent from operating budget, 15 percent from capital funds. The Presbyterian study concluded: ". . . we informally recommend that churches purchase computers that are industry favorites. Also, we stress that churches should look at their needs before they look for hardware." (From The Presbyterian Panel, 1908 Interchurch Center, 475 Riverside Drive, New York, N.Y. 10115-0099.)

Also see Kenneth Bedell, "Which Computer Should Our Church Buy?" *Religion & Media* (May-June 1983) and Kenneth Bedell, "A Printer for the Church," *Church Computer Users Network Newsletter* (Summer 1983).

Appendix A.
Steps in Obtaining
a Computer System

1. *Determine areas where the church needs help with information processing.*

Ask people about tasks they are presently doing that could use computer assistance. Find situations in which it would be helpful to have new information or information organized in new ways. Talk to people with responsibilites in the areas discussed in this book. Ask them whether they feel that computer assistance could help them.

2. *Look at both the long-range and short-range goals of the church.*

Identify ways that computer assistance with information management can help to achieve these goals. Reevaluate the goals in terms of new possibilities open to the church using information processing. Study new possibilities for ministry suggested in this book.

3. *Reexamine computer use in light of the gospel.*

Have the pastor lead the congregation or an appropriate group of the congregation through a process of putting the results of steps one and two into the context of the commitment of the church to be a faithful witness to the gospel. This may change some short-term or even long-term goals. A computer system can bring changes into the operational system of the church on a functional level. It may, in some cases, free people from tedious and repetitive tasks. Or it may increase work by adding the work involved in collecting new information and putting it to use.

4. *Develop a tentative plan of computer use for the church.*

List the possible computer uses in order of priority, including applications suggested in this book that might be used in the future.

5. *Identify the people who can help the church to computerize.*

Some pastors have provided leadership by educating themselves in the uses and availability of equipment and software. They have recommended what to purchase and have helped to set it up and to supervise its use. In other parishes a group of laypeople have worked together to learn about and then install a computer system. Often even when the pastor or others in the parish are well informed, it is wise to hire a consultant who understands both computers and churches. A consultant fulfills the same role that an architect does when a new building is planned. After clarifying the results of steps one through four, the consultant will write specifications for or recommend the purchase of a system to meet the needs. The consultant may also assist with installing the system and training people to use it or making sure that the supplier provides the necessary support.

6. *Meet with the vendor (or vendors) of the software and equipment.*

Include in the meeting not only those who will decide on the purchase but also those who will use the system. Ask the vendor to demonstrate what the computer will do for the church. Listen carefully to make sure that what is being demonstrated is consistent with the uses defined in step four. The careful evaluation of vendors is more important than examining the equipment and the software. Does the system actually do what the vendor says it will? Do the vendors understand questions about the systems and are they able to give clear answers? Do they grasp the needs of the church and will they be able to work with the church to develop future applications?

Ask the vendors for references of other parishes where they have installed computers or find out about other customers if the vendors have not sold to churches. Contact these references to ask whether repairs have been satisfactorily made and the commitments of the vendors have been kept.

Purchasers must clarify where training and continuing support can be obtained if the vendor cannot provide such service as problems arise and new applications are developed. Perhaps the pastor, some parish members, or a consultant can provide such assistance, but before the system is purchased, it is important to be specific about who will be supporting the computer system.

7. *Go ahead.*

Buying a computer system may seem like a great leap of faith, but if the first six steps have been followed, the ministry of the church can begin to benefit from computer use in fulfilling its programs and purposes.

Appendix B.
Tips on Shopping for
a Computer System

1. *Don't buy promises.*

Many dealers and manufacturers, some of them with very good intentions, make promises about computer equipment or software that will soon be available, sometimes with enticements such as a reduced price if the product is purchased unseen. But a parish cannot benefit from a computer system until it is delivered and in operation. It is worth waiting a bit and often spending more money so that equipment can be examined and understood before its purchase.

2. *Never equate cost with quality.*

High cost may reflect a number of things other than quality: low sales volume so that a large profit must be made on each sale, unnecessarily high development or advertising costs, or a low quality product that requires more servicing expense by the vendor. The kingdom of God will not be advanced because a congregation can boast about how much money it spent on a computer system. But at times it may be wise to pay a premium price, such as when the supplier will provide continuing support for the system.

3. *Don't buy more than is needed today.*

Keep an eye on future uses and needs by purchasing equipment which can be expanded, but buy only for immediate use. Both equipment and software will continue to become less expensive, so keep the money in the bank instead of tying it up for several years in equipment that is not yet needed. If, for example, it is thought that eventually three people might need to use the computer at once, be sure to buy a system designed so that it can be expanded to three terminals.

4. *Don't shop for equipment first.*

The quality of software is far more important than the hardware, and the competence and responsibility of the vendor who sells the equipment and software is the most important of all. The very best equipment, coupled with software not well suited to the needs of the church and a vendor who is unable or unwilling to support the computer system, will be of limited use.

5. *Don't assume that a parish cannot use a personal-size computer.*

Some of the first church uses of computers were made by pastors who discovered that information processing was using a large amount of time that could be put to better use. These computers became personal tools for the pastor. Some very big parishes may require systems that are larger than a personal computer, but even the largest congregations will probably find that some tasks can best be done with a personal computer.

6. *Don't trust responsibility for computerization to a single person.*

One person with computer skills may volunteer to take charge of installing the system. A parish would not turn its education program completely over to one person, no matter how gifted and dedicated the person is, without a committee to supervise, receive reports, and be responsible. Yet several parishes have fallen into difficulties by leaving the responsibility for computer purchase or installation to one person without a supervising committee or group. Also, as the computer becomes part of the life of the congregation, it is important that more people become aware of it and know how to use it.

7. *Don't expect immediate results from a computer installation.*

Perhaps a new computer can be used in some ways immediately, but the initial installation and the entering of data into it will take time. And invariably there will be some frustration—as when touching a wrong key by mistake causes data to be lost that took hours to enter or when a person who had hoped to save time immediately must spend an entire day learning to use the equipment. So a congregation should expect a six- to twelve-month period for installing, learning, entering information, and reorganizing church work before a computer becomes integrated into the ongoing life of the parish.